Haunted Ale~
and Northern Virginia

J.J. Smith

4880 Lower Valley Road, Atglen, PA 19310

Other Schiffer Books on Related Subjects
Ghosts! Washington Revisited: The Ghostlore of the Nation's Capital. John Alexander. ISBN: 0764306537. $14.95
Haunted Battlefields: Virginia's Civil War Ghosts. Beth Brown. ISBN: 9780764330575. $14.99
Haunted Richmond. Pamela K. Kinney. ISBN: 9780764327124. $14.95

Designed by John P. Cheek
Type set in Zapf Chancery Bd BT/Zurich BT

ISBN: 978-0-7643-3258-6
Printed in the United States of America

Schiffer Books are available at special discounts for bulk purchases for sales promotions or premiums. Special editions, including personalized covers, corporate imprints, and excerpts can be created in large quantities for special needs. For more information contact the publisher:

Published by Schiffer Publishing Ltd.
4880 Lower Valley Road
Atglen, PA 19310
Phone: (610) 593-1777; Fax: (610) 593-2002
E-mail: Info@schifferbooks.com

For the largest selection of fine reference books on this and related subjects, please visit our
web site at **www.schifferbooks.com**
We are always looking for people to write books on new and related subjects. If you have an idea for a book please contact us at the above address.

This book may be purchased from the publisher.
Include $5.00 for shipping.
Please try your bookstore first.
You may write for a free catalog.

In Europe, Schiffer books are distributed by
Bushwood Books
6 Marksbury Ave.
Kew Gardens
Surrey TW9 4JF England
Phone: 44 (0) 20 8392 8585; Fax: 44 (0) 20 8392 9876
E-mail: info@bushwoodbooks.co.uk
Website: www.bushwoodbooks.co.uk

Dedication

This book is dedicated to my wife Alison. Besides correcting the first draft, she followed me all over Northern Virginia and stood for hours while accompanying me on ghost tours and through graveyards, all the while providing me with encouragement and love. I can't thank her enough.

Acknowledgments

I could not have written this book without the help of several sources of information. Because each provided stories, insights, and personal experience into the spirits of Alexandria and Northern Virginia, I have included a list of those who I feel helped to improve the book, but I take full responsibility for any shortcomings. Thanks to them all.

Alexandria City Hall and Market Square, 301 King Street, Alexandria (703) 838-4000; **www.alexandriava.gov**

Alexandria's Footsteps to the Past Ghost Tour (703) 683-3451

Alexandria Visitors Center at Ramsey House, 221 King Street, Alexandria (703) 838-5005; **www.FunSideofthePotomac.com**

Balls Bluff National Battlefield and Cemetery, Battlefield Parkway, Leesburg, Va. (703) 737-7800

Carlyle House Historic Park, 121 North Fairfax Street, Alexandria (703) 549-2997; **www.carlylehouse.org**

Christ Church, 118 North Washington Street, Alexandria (703) 549-1450

Christmas Attic, 125 South Union Street, Alexandria (703) 548-2829; **www.christmasattic.com**

DC Metro Area Ghost Watchers; **www.dchauntings.com/**

Gadsby's Tavern Museum, 134 North Royal Street, Alexandria (703) 838-4242; **www.gadsbystavern.org**

Ghost & Graveyard Tour, (703) 519-1749; **tours@alexcolonial-tours.com**

Occoquan Inn, 301 Mill Street, Occoquan, Virginia (703) 491-1888; **OccoquanInn@tidalwav.net**

Tomb of the Unknown Soldier of the American Revolution, Old Presbyterian Meeting House, 323 South Fairfax Street, Alexandria (703) 549-6670; **www.opmh.org**

Virginia Scientific Research Association, (which provides ghost tours of Leesburg, Virginia.) (703) 901-8333; **www.vsra.net**

Weems-Botts Museum, Duke and Cameron Streets, Dumfries, Virginia (703) 221-2218; **weems-botts@msn.com**

Woodlawn Plantation, 9000 Richmond Highway, Alexandria, (703) 780-4000; **www.woodlawn1805.org**

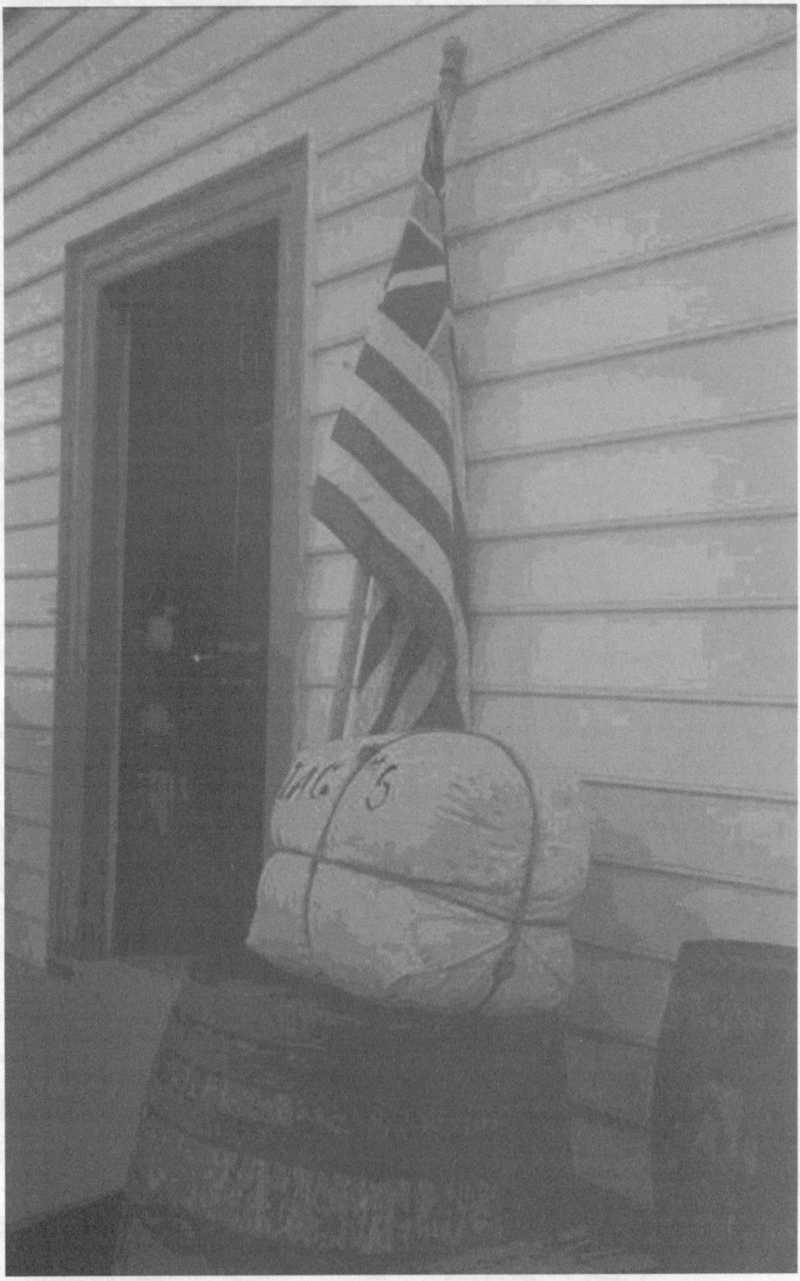

Contents

Foreword... 9

Chapter 1. The Burning Maiden............................... 14
Laura's Presence

Chapter 2. The Christmas Attic................................ 22
Two Spirits Possible

Chapter 3. Gadsby's and the Female Stranger 28
Strangers Arrive • Birth Night Sightings • The Celebrated Mrs. Warren

Chapter 4. The Woodlawn Plantation 38
Well of Spirits

Chapter 5. Legends, Tall Tales, Tragedies and Nightmares.......46
*Introduction and Market Square • The Ramsey House • The John Douglas
Brown House • The Police Station Apparitions • The Voices in the Attic •
The Pirates of Prince Street • The Nightmare House • The Fire Nightmare
• The Pit Nightmare*

Chapter 6. The Carlyle House................................. 64
Roots of Revolution

Chapter 7. D.C. Metro Area Ghost Watchers......................... 70
*A Scent of Roses • The Apparitions and the Lawman • Investigations
• Dangerous Spirits • Belief*

Chapter 8. The Merchant Family and the Weems-Botts House...80
Conversion to a Museum • Mamie's Room • The Colonial Room

Chapter 9. Sex and Death in Occoquan 90
The Fireplace • A List of Occoquan Hauntings

Chapter 10. The Virginia Scientific Research Association..... 98

Chapter 11. I See Dead People 104

  Emotion is the Link

Chapter 12. Hauntings in Leesburg 110

  *The "Seek" Girl • Peek-A-Boo • The Tavern and the Law Firm • Court
  House Ghosts*

Chapter 13. Ball's Bluff Haunting 122

  Colonel Burt

Bibliography.. 126

Foreword
A Historical Perspective of Ghosts & Dead Cats

Do you believe in ghosts? That question elicits a variety of different answers because believing in ghosts means different things to different people. Certainly some people are haunted by their pasts, or their past actions, while others take that question to mean a disembodied spirit or soul, still others have said a ghost could be a "residue energy or a psychic echo" left by a strong emotion. All, or none, of those might be true. What is true is the community of Alexandria, Virginia, located about five miles south of Washington, D.C., and the surrounding Northern Virginia area, is home to some real believers.

Alexandria, founded in 1749 by three Scottish families, is a community steeped in tradition and history dating back to when the town was a colonial seaport. Because it predates the founding of the United States, Alexandria barely raises an eyebrow every July 4th. Its location made it a major center of trade in goods and people as travelers from across the Atlantic Ocean were ferried up the Chesapeake Bay and the Potomac River where they stepped onto the new world at the port of Alexandria. Of course there was no District of Columbia when Alexandria was established, but today the greater D.C. area—generally agreed to be the communities within the Washington Beltway, which rings the city—is considered among the most haunted in the United States.

While Alexandria occupies fifteen square miles of Virginia—framed by Fairfax County to the south and Arlington County in the north and west—it is the area of Alexandria known as Old Town where most of the reported spirit activity occurs. With more than 4,000 historic buildings, many beautiful examples of early American architecture, Old Town Alexandria is one of the most historic communities in the United States. George Washington kept a small home in Alexandria at 508 Cameron Street—a recreation of the house stands there today—and interestingly enough, the house is about a block from one of Alexandria's most famous haunted sites, Gadsby's Tavern, where Washington took his meals when staying at the house. Of further historical note, Gadsby's was host to at least three other U.S. presidents, John Adams, Thomas Jefferson, and James Madison.

Washington, Adams, Jefferson, and Madison are not the only Revolutionary War era heroes to have found themselves in Alexandria. In Washington's case he was a permanent resident, and there is at least one other—little known—hero of the America Revolution who has a permanent home in Alexandria. There is no truer testament to Alexandria's historical significance than the fact that the cemetery immediately behind the Old Presbyterian Meeting House, located at 323 South Fairfax Street, is the final resting place for one of two Unknown Soldiers from the American Revolutionary War (the other is in Philadelphia, Pennsylvania).

While no Civil War battles were fought in, or immediately around Alexandria—which started the war as the most pro-Union city in the south—the city endured a harsh occupation by the Union Army, which drove it to become rabidly pro Confederacy. The Union Army held control of Alexandria mostly because it was one of the few towns in Northern Virginia that had a railroad, and it was used as a staging area to head south, specifically to Manassas, where the First Battle of Bull Run, also known as the First Battle of Manassas, was fought.

The Union Army was so confident going into the battle that they did not prepare medical care for the wounded at the site of the hostilities. They went to Manassas without doctors or nurses, and with no other means of caring for the injured. So wounded Union soldiers were transported back to Alexandria, with the plan of eventually loading them onto trains and moving up north where they would receive full care. Of course many of the men died, but there were so many wounded that local hotels—that had been converted into hospitals—filled up. Once the hotels filled up, there was no place to put the dead, and so bodies were placed on Fairfax Street, all the way down the block. Eventually they ended up stacking the bodies, one on top of the other. In some places the stack grew to be four bodies high and the blood was ankle deep.

John Warfield, the current head of D.C. Metro Area Ghost Watchers (DCMAG), has worked on a case at a residence in Old Town Alexandria, which involved the discovery of body-parts in the basement of a home. Warfield can't give out information on the location—the owner does not want the dwelling to become a tourist attraction—but once the body parts were discovered, DCMAG contacted the Alexandria police. "By law we have to contact the civil authorities once human remains are discovered," he said. "The police investigated, and determined the body parts were at least 100 years old. At that point they lost interest, and recommended we contact the historic society," he added.

After an investigation, Warfield said DCMAG came to the conclusion the body parts were from the Civil War era. "Because we didn't find a full body, but rather arms and legs," he said. During the Civil War, a lot of the houses in Old Town were pressed into service as makeshift hospitals. "My guess is the remains were amputations. In many cases, limbs would be cut off and disposed of in a mass burial site. That's probably what it is," he said. The owner of the house— a woman—contacted DCMAG because she heard knocking from a source she couldn't identify. She didn't know there was a mass burial of amputated limbs on her property, which turns out to not be unusual for DCMAG.

Virginians are proud of their history and tell stories of that history because it says who they are. Tales of ghosts and hauntings are favored among those stories, which is why the book is broken up into two sections. The first section focuses on Alexandria, and the second ventures into Northern Virginia to examine hauntings and ghost stories within a thirty minute drive of Alexandria.

All the history that has occurred in and around Alexandria is the most likely reason Old Town Alexandria has the large concentration of buildings that are active with spirits and ghosts, says Al Tyas, the former head of the DCMAG, who oversaw numerous investigations into Alexandria and Northern Virginia hauntings. Even in times without strife the Old Town area was full of taverns and brothels, it was a very rough area and people were killed there, Tyas said. In addition, the area was not very sanitary and the buildings—most constructed as row houses resulting in an entire block burning down—are so close to each other that plagues and outbreaks of small pox or typhoid fever were the norm, he said. What that has to do with ghosts is that a lot of people died young and very quickly, Tyas adds. The historical events that occurred which led to the deaths of so many people in such a small area made Alexandria a place where buildings are susceptible to haunting, he said.

Founders and Dead Cats

As mentioned earlier, Alexandria was founded by three families. They are:

The Alexanders, (brothers John and Philip signed the agreement for the Alexander family which ceded land for the incorporation of the town that was then named for the family).

The Ramseys (William and Anne) whose home—the oldest in Alexandria—is located at 221 King Street. The house is now the Alexandria Visitors Center and there are claims it too is haunted.

The Carlyles (John and Sarah), whose house, an eighteenth century Georgian Palladian style mansion, still stands at 121 North Fairfax Street and today is a museum operated by the Northern Virginia Park Authority. This house is also claimed to be haunted.

While John and Sarah Carlyle are known as one of the founding families of Alexandria, what is not so well known is that the Carlyles were very superstitious, to the point that they installed a defense against ghosts. What is interesting about this is the Carlyles were not as concerned about human intruders in their home as they were about spirit intruders. During the colonial era of America, it was not unusual for homes like the Carlyle mansion to be equipped with a home security system called "a busybody." The busybody system of security was a surveillance system consisting of tin panels stuck out from windows, which could mirror the outside of homes. Dwellings that had a busybody usually had one mounted at the front entrance so the inhabitants could see who was knocking and decide if they wanted to answer or not. It also allowed the homeowner to monitor the property. Curiously enough, considering the grandness of their home, the Carlyles did not have the busybody system, indicating they were not afraid of possible human intruders, yet they were so afraid of ghosts they installed a defense to keep spirits out.

They did not want their house haunted at all, either during their lifetime or afterwards, so they implemented a Scottish superstition to defend against ghosts and bad luck, which directs that burying a dead cat somewhere in a home prevents specters from taking up residence there. For 200 years no one ever imagined the Carlyles would have buried a dead cat in their home, but in 1976, during America's Bicentennial, the truth became known when local historians began restoration of the Carlyle house in preparation for its conversion to a museum. When restoration began, some of the old walls had to be torn down so repairs on the house could take place. When one such wall was torn down, the skeleton of a dead cat was discovered. The historians concluded that the remains were not those of a cat that was ill and somehow fell or crawled into the wall to die, because the cat was carefully mummified. It was wrapped in cloth and placed in its own little coffin before being entombed in a wall near the front door. Museum officials have re-interred the cat's remains at Carlyle house, so the building is being protected from ghosts by a dead cat. As it turns out, you can't swing a dead cat in Old Town Alexandria—or other parts of Northern Virginia—without hitting a ghost story, so for those who live in that area, burying a deceased feline in their homes may not be a bad idea.

Chapter

1

The Burning Maiden

Many of the institutions that reside in Alexandria—like the buildings they occupy—are as old, or nearly as old, as the town itself. That includes the newspaper *The Alexandria Gazette* (now publishing under the name *The Alexandria Gazette Packet*), which has been reporting on Alexandria since 1785. But it is an issue published in 1868 that is both shocking and interesting. Included in the Monday, June 29, 1868, edition of the *Gazette* there are notices of community events, personal milestones, and crime. The more mundane notices include:

A schedule of readings "of a selection of works by Charles Dickens" by the "rich, flexible voice" of F.C. Bang.

An account of the first sermons preached by Revs. Messrs. G.E. Peterkin and Kinloch Nelson, "gentlemen upon whom Deacon's orders were conferred on Friday last."

And a report of a seven-year prison sentence imposed on George W. Payne for horse theft.

But there is also a news story headlined "Fatal and Melancholy Affair," which tells of how Laura M. Schafer, twenty-six, was so badly burned two days earlier in an accident which occurred at 107 North Fairfax Street, that she died of her wounds. The first paragraph of the *Gazette* story—known among journalists as the lead—says:

On Saturday evening last, about half-past seven o'clock a deplorable accident occurred to Miss Laura M. Schafer, the youngest, and a beautiful daughter of Mr. Christian Schafer, the well known and highly respected confectioner of Fairfax street, which has suddenly and horribly deprived the city of one of its prettiest ornaments, and a family and large circle of friends of one of their most cherished members; and incidentally, has been the occasion of another death, more horrible, from the fact of its being an act of self-destruction.

The events of June 27, 1868, that led to the death of Laura Schaffer started as a mission of family care for Laura,

107 North Fairfax Street, Alexandria, where Laura Schafer met a horrible fate.

who was looking after her eighty-year-old grandmother, [only identified in the *Gazette* as Mrs. Ballenger]. After getting her grandmother tucked in for the night, Laura was dressing for the evening in her own room—on the second floor—when she dropped a kerosene lamp which shattered, splattering kerosene everywhere, including onto Laura's dress. The lamp's wick was lit and it ignited the kerosene on her dress. Laura Schaffer tried to get out of her room, but the front door was jammed because of humidity. She ran to the second floor window and screamed for help as flames engulfed her dress. After screaming for help, she again tried her bedroom door and this time it opened. By then she was totally engulfed by the flames—witnesses said the flames "extended far above her head"—and she tumbled down the stairs to the front door. Laura's brother in law—William Phillips—happened to be outside at the time, and he heard the screaming. Mr. Phillips rushed into the home and covered Laura in an attempt to extinguish the flames. Unfortunately his efforts were too late. She was too badly burned and died the next morning, June 28, 1868.

Laura had been engaged for five years and one day. The dress she was wearing when she dropped the kerosene lamp was her wedding dress and she was trying it on in anticipation of her nuptials. She died on what would have been her wedding day and the ghost of Laura Schaffer remains at 107 Fairfax Street, and might be reliving the horrors of the night she burned.

Laura's Presence

The building at 107 Fairfax Street is no longer a home. The property, located in the heart of Old Town Alexandria across the street from Market Square, is too valuable a spot for it to remain a dwelling. Therefore it has been transformed into a business facility. One of the businesses that occupied 107 Fairfax Street was a real estate office. A few years ago, on a June night, one of the real estate agents was working late. The agent's office was located on the first floor, and she

Engulfed in flames, Laura Schafer tumbled down these stairs screaming for help.

heard something not only coming from upstairs, but from the area that was Laura's bedroom. Naturally the real estate agent wanted to find out what the noise was, so she ventured to the second floor to find the door to that room closed. But the door wasn't only closed, when she tried to open the door, she found it was jammed. And not only was the door jammed, when she put her hand against the wood, she found the door was hot. Now she believed that there was a fire in the room, and stepped away from the door, when it suddenly burst open, but no one emerged from the room. However, she felt an intense heat rush past her.

Not long after that incident, the real estate company sold the building and a retail business—called A House in the Country—set up shop at the location. A House in the Country sold Christmas decorations and ornaments. While no adults have seen the ghost of Laura Schaffer, she is reported to have been seen by small children accompanying adults to the store who have asked "who is the woman in the white dress?"

Today, the building is occupied by the high-end candy store, Candi's Candies, which seems appropriate since Laura's father—Christian Schafer—was a "well known and highly respected confectioner." Candida Krbb is the owner of Candi's Candies and has occupied the building since 2007. During the first year of opening the business, Ms. Krbb reports having a strange experience in the basement of the building.

"I don't believe in ghosts. I figured that when you died, that's it. You die and you're gone forever," Ms. Krbb said. However, not long after setting up shop in the building, Ms. Krbb said she had strange experience. "I went to the basement to get a bag. I went down the stairs fine, but as soon as I reached the bottom and turned to get what I went down there for, oh my God, I felt something was there," she said. "My whole body got goose bumps, my eyes became teary and I was thinking, oh my God, something is here. It wasn't Laura, it was something else. Somehow I pictured a man. I didn't see anything, but I was petrified, and when I got back up on the first floor, I showed everyone who was here my arms, and they could see how watery my eyes had gotten," Ms. Krbb said.

Ms. Krbb's friends and colleagues advised her to "never go into the basement again." But Ms. Krbb has. "What it was down there, I don't know, but there is definitely something down there. I'm not afraid of Laura, but the basement was spooky. I'd like to know what happened in the basement. Something happened. It was very, very, very scary. I don't know what happened. I even said to the ghost investigators [the DC Metro Area Ghost Watchers, DCMAG, who conducted investigations at the site] that the spirit in the basement is a man. At a minimum, Ms. Krbb is convinced that the spirit in the basement is not that of Laura Schafer, because she believes she had contact with Laura. "The first time I smelled burning. When I smelled the burning smell, I checked around to see if anyone was smoking, but nothing. The next night the same thing happened. I smelled a burning smell and I thought 'where is that burning smell coming from?' I checked again to see where the smell was coming from. I especially want to know if there is heat or fire smoldering somewhere in the building, but I looked around and everything was fine. As I checked, I wasn't thinking about Laura Schafer at all. It wasn't until about twenty minutes after I finished looking around that I thought that the smell had something to do with Laura Schafer. It was exciting. I wasn't afraid; it was exciting. The only experiences I had were the burning smell and the day I felt a presence in the basement. There haven't been any other strange experiences since," Ms Krbb said.

In addition, a few days after the basement incident, a woman entered Candi's Candies and requested to speak with Ms. Krbb. "She said, 'I've got to talk to you.'" The woman claimed to have worked in the building for a year, and that there's something in the basement. "I couldn't believe it," just a few days after an experience in the basement a stranger approached me to warn me, "There is something in the basement, no doubt about it," Ms. Krbb said.

Because people report having heard a woman say "hello," DCMAG's investigations at 107 Fairfax Street included "electronic voice phenomena" (EVP). According to the American Association of Electronic Voice Phenomena, EVP is unexpected voices heard in recording media and might be a form of after-death communication. But it didn't work out exactly like the typical EVP experience, said Al Tyas, the former head of DCMAG who oversaw the investigation. When the building was still a Christmas store, the Ghost Watchers held an "EVP session where we asked [Laura Schafer] for a sign to make her presence known," he said. There were Christmas stockings close by that had lights attached to them, and once we made the request "the lights suddenly started blinking," he said. "No one was near them [the stockings]," he said. In addition, one of the investigators actually smelled burning while standing near the stairs, but "it was nowhere near the top floor, where the burning primarily occurred," he said. "People were in the lounge. That was unusual," he added.

Chapter

2

The Christmas Attic

At the corner of South Union and Prince Streets in Old Town Alexandria, about 150 feet from the Potomac River, sits a building that was formerly used as a shipping warehouse, but has since been converted into a retail facility. The Christmas Attic, which specializes in Christmas ornaments and decorations, has occupied the property at 125 South Union Street since 1971, but that is just a drop in the life of the building which was constructed in

The warehouse turned retail outlet at 125 South Union Street, Old Town Alexandria.

1785 by Capt. John Harper, a former sea captain who settled in Alexandria and who so prospered in trade and commerce that he built an entire block of houses on Prince Street between South Union and Lee Streets as dowries for his daughters.

John Harper and his first wife Dorothy were a very loving couple, and by age thirty-nine, Dorothy Harper had given birth to twenty children, including two sets of twins. When Dorothy Harper stopped producing children it was because she was ill and she died three years later at age forty-two. Captain Harper was heartbroken over the death of Dorothy, but time healed his wounds and a few years later he married Mary Cunningham, who he had nine more children with. In total Captain Harper had twenty-nine children, but the mortality rate during the colonial era was about forty percent and twenty-one of the Harper children survived into adulthood. However, all twenty-one were daughters and when those girls reached marrying age, their father was obligated to provide each of them with a dowry that would be presented to the groom on the wedding day. With twenty-one girls and twenty-one dowries there were also twenty-one weddings and receptions that had to be paid for. It was a problem for Captain Harper, but certainly not a huge dilemma for a man who, during the revolution procured for General Washington eight casks of powder, drums, and colors enough for five Virginia companies, and who would later help lay the cornerstone of the U.S. Capitol along with George Washington. Such a man would not let a matter as trivial as dowries deter the happiness of his more than a score of daughters. Captain Harper found the answer in real estate, specifically on Prince Street which runs east to west adjacent to his warehouse. There were several empty parcels of land available on Prince Street, and Captain Harper purchased enough to build twenty-one houses, thereby creating both the needed dowries and the 100 block of Prince Street, which is now known as "Captain's Row."

Two Spirits Possible

While Captain Harper lived a colorful enough life to be of interest, it is his warehouse, and the possibility that two spirits might haunt the building that is the focus of this chapter. The spirits are identified as a male adult and possibly a small boy, and both the building's current occupants and the DC Metro Area Ghost Watchers (DCMAG) have made attempts to find out the truth.

The popular story is that the building is haunted by a sea captain, says Diana Bridger, assistant manager of the Christmas Attic. Obviously that's because a sea captain constructed the building, says Ms. Bridger, who has been with the store for seven years. The story that is most repeated is the captain's young wife went to England and she never returned. Supposedly, from time to time he can be seen in the fourth floor window looking out at the river waiting for her to return, but that does not fit with any of the facts of Captain Harper's life, she said. Also ghost investigators have examined the building and they do not believe the spirit to be that of a sea captain; they believe it to be someone who is from the 1940s, and possibly he is named "Jack," but no one is sure. Nonetheless, one of the investigators actually saw the ghost, Ms. Bridger said. And, so far, the investigator is the only one who has been on the property and who claims to have actually seen the ghost, she said. That was in 2003, during an investigation by DCMAG. One of the investigators was exceptionally sensitive, she said. However, the rest of the investigators could also feel a presence, and that's where the name "Jack" came from, she added.

Over a five year period there have been about a dozen investigations at the site, partly because the Christmas Attic cooperates, and the veteran ghost investigators like to use the building as a training area for new members of the group, Ms. Bridger said. The investigation included attempts at obtaining "electronic voice phenomena" (EVP) and the group believes it has been successful, she said. The investigators set up a tape recorder in the store's office with the lights out, at least two others with cassette recorders, and the group's leader would start a conversation, she said. "The conversations were always very respectful, with such questions as 'can you make yourself known?' and then they would pause," she said. "It wasn't séance-like, but more like a conversation," she added. And then, on at least one recording the question is put to the spirit, "why are you still here?" and there is a possible response, a whisper saying, "don't know," she said. However, Ms. Bridger says she has heard the recording and is not sure about the alleged response. "I couldn't make out the 'don't know', but I could hear a change in that tape," she said. Nonetheless, all the investigators always felt something, she added. "They always felt the presence was not far, in a doorway, near where they were conducting the conversation," she said.

John Warfield, the head of DCMAG, said the Christmas Attic does seem to be haunted by a male spirit. "It seems to be a fairly nice haunting. We call him Mr. Jack because we can't figure out why he's there, because [as best as DCMAG can ascertain] there's no reason for that place to be haunted. We haven't been able to figure out why a ghost would take up residence there," Warfield said. The ghost does talk to us at times, and I've asked him to give up his name, but he won't. At first we thought he was a seaman, but through our research we've found that not to be the case.

In addition, during one of the EVP sessions, the ghost grabbed a hold of Mr. Warfield's hair, and pulled. "I was so surprised that I said, 'That didn't just happen!' I just let it go and after the EVP session I reviewed the tape of the session, the ghost was asked to communicate with us, you can hear the words 'can't talk,' and that's when my hair was pulled," he said. "I had the experience of having my hair pulled backed up by the tape," he said. In addition, whenever DCMAG conducts EVP sessions at the Christmas Attic, the tapes keeps picking up bells that are jingling in the store, Warfield said. The EVP sessions are always conducted when the store is closed, so there aren't any customers, yet we hear bells jingling in one area of the building and we can't find any reason for it, he added.

In addition, the investigators are not the only people to feel a presence at the building, Ms. Bridger said. Christmas Attic employees have had encounters with the ghost. "We've had a few employees who…one young boy, who felt like he was almost pushed at the top of the attic stairs once. I do believe him, because he didn't say anything about it for two weeks after the incident.

Gadsby's Tavern, located at 134 North Royal Street, Old Town, has gone by various names throughout its history. Now known as Gadsby's Tavern Museum, it consists of two buildings, the tavern, built in 1785, and the City Hotel, built in 1792. It was originally known as Wise's Tavern because it was owned by John Wise, the tavern king of Alexandria, but the buildings are named for Englishman John Gadsby who operated them from 1796 to 1808, and "put the tavern on the map," according to Emily Soapes, a docent at Gadsby's museum.

Gadsby made the tavern famous by a combination of hard work—he was proud of the accommodations the tavern provided, it had the reputation as one of the best places to eat and drink— and by turning the tavern into a center of political, business and social life in early Alexandria. It can be compared to today's conference centers, Soapes said.

Gadsby's was so well thought of, when George Washington bought a home in Old Town—located at 508 Cameron Street—to provide him with a place to stay while he was in town conducting business, he was sure to buy a house as close to Gadsby's as

Gadsby's Tavern at 134 North Royal Street, Old Town Alexandria.

possible. The dwelling Washington purchased is about a block from the tavern and a refurbished version of the house stands there today. In addition to Washington, other famous guests of the period included Thomas Jefferson, who attended a banquet at Gadsby's ballroom immediately following his inauguration as president; the Marquis de Lafayette, who reviewed troops from the tavern's steps; John Adams; and James Madison.

Because Washington was such a frequent guest of the tavern, John Gadsby saw an opportunity, and in 1797 he instituted the "Birth Night Ball" in honor of George Washington's birthday. During Washington's retirement years, Gadsby was even able to persuade the former president to attend the Birth Night Ball. However, Gadsby relinquished ownership of the tavern in 1808, and with the change in ownership the ball was discontinued until 1932 when it was revived, leading to one of the most famous ghost sightings in Alexandria's history. However, before we turn to this twentieth century famous sighting, we will go back to 1816.

Strangers Arrive

In 1816, when this well documented story took place, Gadsby's was no longer known as Gadsby's. It was known as "the City Hotel." In September of 1816, a sailing vessel of medium size dropped anchor just off the dock of Alexandria. The ship did not fly any international colors, or have a name painted on it, or have any indication of its identity. While that was not illegal at the time, it was unusual. In addition, the ships officers did not go through customs at the dock, rather the crew simply put down a boat, into which six seamen and an officer boarded, along with two passengers and some luggage. The two passengers were a young man and woman and the boat was rowed to the dock, where the seamen unloaded the baggage, the officer helped the young man and woman out of the boat, removed his hat, bowed deeply to the couple, returned to the boat, and rowed back to the ship.

The young man went to the harbor master and said he and his wife had to interrupt their journey because she was ill and he needed a place for her to convalesce. The harbormaster recommended the City Tavern. The couple then ventured to the tavern, where they were met by the wife of one of the two proprietors at the door. The young man explained why they were there, and Dr. Samuel Richardson was summoned. The proprietor's wife then showed them to room number eight, on the second floor, which is now always referred to as the strangers' room. That the couple would get a private room is very unusual, because during that period, guests who stayed at the tavern did not rent a room. In fact a guest did not even rent a bed for himself because up to five people might rent space in the same bed. What a guest did rent was clean sheets for the bed. Therefore, the fact that the couple could obtain a private room might be testament to either their standing in society, or the tavern owners' fear that the female stranger's illness was contagious. While local legend says the couple stayed in room eight, Ms. Soapes says the museum does not know exactly which bedchamber the Female Stranger may have occupied. Even though wealthier guests had access to luxury accommodations, in most cases they were still only renting a bed.

Once the couple was shown to their room, the story took a second strange turn. The young man had Dr. Richardson and the tavern keepers sworn to secrecy as to the identities of the two guests. To this day, it is not known who they were.

The young man and the woman stayed in the room, but instead of recuperating, she steadily got sicker. The young man would venture out of the room a few times, mostly for meals in the tavern, and he went to the apothecary to get prescriptions for his wife and things she needed. But he mostly stayed in the room. At the same time, the whole town was talking about the couple, with the big question being "who are these people?"

They also asked, "How is she doing?" The answer to that was she was not doing well. She died in that room on October 14, 1816, and she is buried in St. Paul's Church Cemetery, located near the corner of Wilkes and Hamilton Streets. She is buried under a very expensive stone slab—costing $1,500 in 1816, which was an enormous amount of money at the time—resting on six elaborately carved stone pillars (other raised slabs in the cemetery sit on plain rectangular blocks). The slab has an inscription that is divided into three parts. The top of the inscription is an epitaph, followed by a short verse, and finally a line from the Acts of the Apostles. It reads:

> To the memory of a *FEMALE STRANGER* [in all capital letters, that is why today she is called the Female Stranger], *whose mortal sufferings terminated on the 14th Day of October 1816, aged 23 years and 8 months. This stone was placed here by her disconsolate husband in whose arms she sighed out her last breath and who, under God, did his utmost even to soothe the cold dead fear of death.*
>
> *How loved, how valued once avails thee not, to whom related, or to whom begot, a heap of dust alone remains of thee, tis all thou are, and all that the proud shall be.*
>
> *To him gave all the prophets witness that through his name, whosoever believeth in him shall receive remission of sins. Acts 10th Chapter, 13th Verse*

Shortly after the funeral, the young man disappeared. He left behind a large number of unpaid debts, including payment for the tombstone, for Dr. Richardson's services, and payment for the bill at the City Tavern. Despite leaving such large debts, no one involved ever revealed who the man claimed he and the young woman were. However, there is much speculation, including that she was a relative of Napoleon Bonaparte, who had met his final defeat at Waterloo in June 1815, and that she was on the run from European authorities who had been hunting down and jailing Bonaparte's relatives.

There is also speculation that she was Aaron Burr's—the third vice president under Thomas Jefferson—daughter, Theodosia, who disappeared with the schooner "Patriot," which set sail from Georgetown, South Carolina, on December 30, 1812, and was never heard from again. Others speculate that the two strangers were tragic victims of incest who were a brother and sister separated very young, but who did not discover that they were siblings until after they were married.

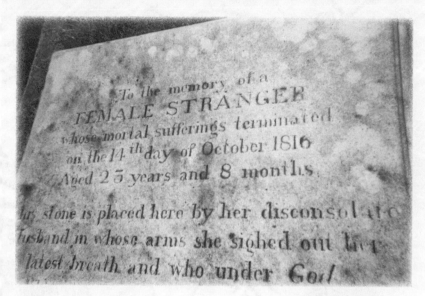

The Female Stranger's grave. After nearly 200 years the slab's text is easily readable, testifying to the high quality, and expense, of the stone carving.

Birth Night Sightings

In 1915, the last paying guest left the hotel that was operating in the building. After the end of the hotel period, the building was used for shops, as an auction house, and a boarding house.

In 1932, the decision was made to restore Gadsby's, and along with a revived tavern, it was decided to reinstate the Birth Night Ball, which now takes place in February, usually the weekend closest to George Washington's birthday. Ball guests can mingle with costumed interpreters who portray the Washingtons and other famous figures of the Revolutionary period, as well as enjoy period-inspired food, and dance in the eighteenth century style in the historic ballroom. The first revived ball was such a big event at the time, that it was broadcast over the radio. It is not known how many sightings of a woman believed to be the Female Stranger occurred prior to the return of the

Birth Night Ball, but during the revived ball, an Alexandria woman said she saw—in the ballroom—a young woman, who she described as having an oval face, very pale complexion, long black hair, and a look of inconsolable sadness. The young woman was not speaking to anyone, and she did not seem to be noticed by most of the attendees. According to the Alexandria woman, the young woman looked as solid as anyone; she was not hazy nor a smoky apparition. The Alexandria woman said the young woman was wearing nineteenth century traveling clothes, specifically a dove gray traveling coat, trimmed in black, and a traveling hat with black gloves. The Alexandria woman wanted to know why the woman was allowed into the ball wearing a costume from the wrong period, but she turned her attention back to the dance. On her way out she asked who the woman in the wrong period costume was, and she was told she must have seen the Female Stranger.

The second known sighting of the Female Stranger at a Birth Night Ball was recorded fifteen years later. By then, lots of Alexandrians knew about the Stranger. This second sighting was made by a local businessman. He was having fun at the ball when he saw a woman who resembled the description of the Stranger. She was standing by a door. As he walked towards her, he lost sight of her in the crowd and never found her again.

In 1961 there was a third sighting of the Female Stranger at the Birth Night Ball. The witness was a guest from New Jersey, but despite being from another state, he was very familiar with Alexandria and its stories. There was a Washington's Day Parade, and many colonial re-enactors were in Alexandria for the parade, and the gentleman was one of those re-enactors. While at the ball, the re-enactor said he saw the woman—who seemed out of place—in the same spot as previous sightings. Because he knew the stories associated with the Female Stranger, he resolved not to let the woman out of his sight as he walked across the room—right through the dancers. He never took his eyes off the woman. As he made it halfway across the ballroom, the woman, who he described as very sad, turned and walked into the corridor without giving any sign she had seen him coming, and without appearing alarmed by his direct stare and approach. By that time he was close enough to almost catch up to her, as he entered the corridor, he saw her turn into room number 8. He followed her into the guest room (which Gadsby's currently leaves open so tourists can see what the accommodations were like during the colonial era), but there was no one there. However, there was a problem. On the bedside table was a candle lamp that was lit and sitting close to the edge of the table. Untended flames are never left to burn in any of Old Town's historic buildings, because the wood is so dry that it can burn like paper. So there is a real concern about open flames. The gentleman knew immediately that the flame should not be lit and left untended, so he turned back to the ballroom and found the "master of the ball"—the person in charge of running the ball for that year. He told the master of the ball that he was just in the Strangers' room and there was a candle burning there.

The master of the ball indicated there shouldn't be a candle burning and it needed to be extinguished. So they returned to the Strangers room, and the candle lamp was still at the edge of the table, but the candle was not lit. In fact the candle had never burned. It had a white wick. The man from New Jersey insisted that the candle had been burning moments before. As they turned to leave the room, the master of the ball reached out to push the lamp back to the center of the table and drew back his hand covered with burn blisters on four of his fingers.

Today, Gadsby's is both a museum and working restaurant in which the wait staff is dressed in colonial era costumes, and colonial era food is on the menu. It has been a while since there has been a Birth Night appearance of the Female Stranger, and when asked about the Stranger, most docents and employees of Gadsby's will give the same reply, "There aren't any ghosts in Gadsby's."

During a tour of Gadsby's, Emily Soapes said, "I've been in here by myself and haven't run into one [ghost]." In addition, Gadsby's is like any old building, it creaks "making it a great setting for a ghost story," she said.

While it might make a good setting for a ghost story, Gadsby's denies there is a ghost and it does not allow anyone to investigate, says Al Tyas, the former head of DC Ghost Watchers. Gadsby's is very much against any investigation in the tavern and museum and they do not even like to discuss it. While talking with a manager at Gadsby's, "I mentioned the 'G' word and they got very defensive about it, and she said, 'there are no ghosts here'," Tyas said. "I think, they believe they'll get a bunch of Satan worshipers if they admit to the presence of a spirit," he added. There is some irony to not allowing ghost investigations "because the staff has had encounters and we [ghost watchers] just get bits and pieces of it," he said. When it happens, Gadsby's tries to cover it up as best they can, because they refuse to admit there is anything going on there, he said.

Tyas has been to the Female Stranger's grave and found something unusual. "The grave is raised. It's on a slab on six pillars maybe two feet high," he said. "Someone keeps going by and putting rocks on top of it, which is interesting because it's a Jewish custom."

On Gadsby's itself, John Warfield, the current head of D.C. Metro Area Ghost Watchers, has a somewhat different perspective. While the tavern is noted to be active with spirits, few of the restaurant's patrons or museum visitors experience anything unusual, he said. Therefore it's likely "this place can be filed as a place with great food, and no ghosts," he added.

The Celebrated Mrs. Warren

Christ Church Graveyard, located at 118 North Washington Street, was completed by 1768, and in use at least five years before Christ Church, which was under construction from 1767 to 1773 by John Carlyle. It was the Anglican Church prior to the Revolution, so it was the "established church," and counted George Washington among its vestry, and was the confirmation site of Robert E. Lee. Hundreds of people were buried in the graveyard. Between 1789 and 1798, one of the few continuous periods for which good records remain, over 400 remains were interred in the cemetery and forty-three percent of them were younger than twelve. Among those resting at Christ Church Graveyard is Anne Warren, or the "Celebrated Mrs. Warren," who died in Alexandria on June 28, 1808, at thirty-nine.

She was an English lady who married an American and they lived in Philadelphia, where she gained fame as an actress, hence the title "Celebrated." She and her husband operated a successful drama touring company. She was on a tour of the South, giving "dramatic readings and recitations," when she suddenly left the earth. She was performing her one-woman show at Gadsby's ballroom, because it was one of the larger venues able to accommodate Mrs. Warren, and she had recited Cleopatra's death scene from Shakespeare's "Anthony & Cleopatra," when she mimed clutching the asp to her chest, and fell back onto the divan. The audience applauded, but Mrs. Warren was not able to take any bows for she was dead. Despite being a Philadelphian, she is buried in Christ Church Graveyard and some people believe, because she was not able to take her bows, Mrs. Warren today haunts Gadsby's, along with the Female Stranger.

Gadsby's and the Female Stranger

Chapter

4

The Woodlawn Plantation

Hidden among the strip malls and fast food franchises that line Richmond Highway (Route 1) south of Old Town Alexandria is Woodlawn Plantation. Hidden it is, for visitors who turn off of Route 1 onto the plantation's private road will find the mansion does not immediately materialize. Like the ghost stories associated with the huge house, visitors will find they have to negotiate a winding tree-lined back road. However, such visitors are implored to keep going because both a tour of the house, and the ghost experiences and sightings—told by the staff with some encouragement—are worth the trip.

Located at 9000 Richmond Highway, Alexandria, the Woodlawn Plantation is near George Washington's home in Mount Vernon—which is three miles away and can be seen from the side of the plantation that views the Potomac River—because in 1799 former President Washington gave 2,000 acres of land to Major Lawrence Lewis (George Washington's nephew) and Eleanor "Nelly" Custis Lewis (Martha Washington's granddaughter; Mrs. Washington was a widow when she married George) as a wedding gift. Eleanor Custis and her brother George Washington

The Woodlawn Plantation, 9000 Richmond Highway, Alexandria.

Park Custis were raised by Martha Washington, and as wards and heirs of the president the siblings were well known during Washington's administrations in New York and Philadelphia. Eleanor and George Custis were also immortalized in Edward Savage's painting *Washington Family*.

It was during President Washington's retirement that he called for his nephew, Major Lawrence Lewis, to serve as his personal secretary. Major Lewis, who hailed from Fredericksburg, Virginia, entered into military service in 1794, helped suppress the "Whiskey Rebellion," and would serve as aide-de-camp to General Daniel Morgan. When Washington ended his service as president, he recruited several of his nephews to assist him at Mount Vernon, including Lewis. As Washington's secretary, Lewis was expected to entertain visitors and guests who came to Mount Vernon to meet and pay homage to the first president. During the time of Lawrence's employment at Mount Vernon, he and Eleanor met and shortly thereafter announced their engagement. The two were married at Mount Vernon on February 22, 1799, Washington's last birthday. As a testament to the regard Washington had for Lewis, the former president named his nephew as primary executor of his will, a task Major Lewis spent the rest of his life implementing.

Following the deaths of the former President and Mrs. Martha Washington, the Lewis family undertook construction of the Woodlawn Plantation in 1800, which was designed by Dr. William Thornton, architect of the U.S. Capitol. The house was built in sections. The north and south wings were completed first, and the main middle section was completed in 1805. As soon as the house was complete, the plantation became an active social center in postcolonial America. Visitors were entertained on a lavish scale by the first president's closest family members. Lawrence and Eleanor had eight children, but only three survived to adulthood, Frances Parke, Lorenzo, and Angela. The children enjoyed visits, parties and balls with their cousins at Arlington House and Tudor Place and were educated in Philadelphia, New Haven, and Alexandria. Like their benefactors, Lawrence and Eleanor doted on their children and subsequent grandchildren, passing on the material possessions given to them by their ancestors. In addition, to honor their uncle and grandmother, the Lewis' placed numerous likenesses of the Washingtons throughout their home and preserved a collection of family related articles that they would use and share with their guests. The Lewis' would give a guest a swatch of cloth or a button off a garment worn by the president and Mrs. Washington, or a signature cut from a letter. During its first forty years, Woodlawn was host to presidents, explorers, military heroes, and world travelers, including the Marquis de Lafayette, who included a stop at the Woodlawn Plantation on his "farewell tour" of the United States.

In the 1820s, a twenty-six-year-old niece of the Lewis' was visiting Woodlawn Plantation when she became ill and died within a twenty-four hour period succumbing to her illness before her parents arrived. Coincidentally, her death occurred around the same time the Lewis' lost their fifteen-year-old daughter, Agnes, also to a sudden illness, in Philadelphia where she was going to school. In addition, the year of 1839 dealt Nelly a double blow as both Major Lewis and her daughter Angela died. The deaths were so devastating to Nelly that she left Woodlawn to live on her son Lorenzo's estate. Woodlawn was eventually inherited by Lorenzo, who put it up for sale in 1846.

At the same time Woodlawn was put up for sale, Quaker timber scouts were searching for mature oak trees to supply Joseph Gillingham's, a prominent Philadelphia Quaker, shipbuilding operation. Gillingham purchased all 2,000 acres of the Woodlawn Estate and another 1,000 acres of neighboring Mount Vernon Estate. In addition to supplying timber for the shipbuilding operation, the plantation's fertile soil and healthy climate allowed the Quaker families to found a farming community without slave labor, following their belief that such a venture could be economically sound as well as ethically right.

Woodlawn eventually was acquired by U.S. Senator Oscar Wilder Underwood, a Democrat representing Alabama. When

Underwood retired from the Senate in 1926, he sought the quiet of Woodlawn, where he took up writing. Underwood died on January 25, 1929, in an upstairs bedroom, but, despite the deaths of the Lewis' niece and Senator Underwood, there does not seem to be a single event, or death, that is undeniably linked to any haunting activity at the plantation. For some reason, the niece and Underwood are not considered as strong ghost candidates as Laura Schafer or the Female Stranger are at the Old Town locations. However, those working at the plantation and who do not want to be named, says other likely candidates for the haunting of the house are the scores of slaves who lived and died on the plantation. According to the census figures collected during the Lewis' tenure at Woodlawn, for every twenty-five whites engaged in agriculture there were ninety-one slaves so engaged.

The enslaved population served as field hands and laborers, but also as skilled seamstresses, blacksmiths, and cooks, and in other refined duties. However, surviving documents only provide limited information about the slaves at Woodlawn, and mostly only in relation to their work. For example, "Sukey," a seamstress, oversaw the stitching completed by other slaves, while "Doll" and "Dolcey" were two slaves that worked in the laundry. "Hanson," a male slave, served as the cook for the household, preparing meals for the Lewis family and their guests, according to docents, who are very well versed in the history of the house. Again, it was the slave population that provides Woodlawn with a possible source of spirits that haunt the house and the wells underneath.

Well of Spirits

"We have the well," says a docent who leads tours through the mansion. Because "spirits [were believed to] come out of the water, the well is kept closed." Actually, there are two wells, one directly outside the house on the south side and the other in the basement. African slaves believed water was a means for spirits to travel. The wells are kept covered now. If this is to prevent spirits from entering the house, it is too late.

The plantation's outer well. Both the well in the home's basement and the outer well are believed to be conduits for spirits that move through water.

While the house's wells are in the basement and on the grounds a few feet from the house, Woodlawn staff and visitors have reported encounters with plantation spirits all through the house, including on the second floor and in the attic. Words, names, and other noises have been reported. One staff member said someone called her name when she was the only one in the house; another staffer reported hearing a baby cry when she was the only one in the dwelling.

Another strange incident involved a baby who needed a diaper changed. The mother changed the baby and set the infant down and turned away from the baby to deal with the diaper. When the mother turned back to her baby, the infant had been moved to the top of a nearby dresser.

At Woodlawn, children have been sensitive to the presence of spirits. A docent told of a little girl who was part of a tour who looked into the attic and said, "There's a man up there." A quick search of the attic found no one.

In a separate incident, a little boy who was on a tour refused to enter an upstairs bedroom, and children are not the only tour members who have refused to enter a room. Adults have declined to enter "the apartment room" on the second floor where Senator Underwood died. After refusing to enter the apartment room, a female tourist said to a docent, "The room gives me the heebie jeebies."

While paranormal investigators have sought to conduct investigations at Woodlawn, the National Trust for Historic Preservation, which owns the house now, does not allow organized investigations of the structure. Rather, the paranormal investigators who have conducted examinations at Woodlawn have done so on an ad hoc basis while on tours. One thing investigators have done is to take photographs, a practice that is not allowed in the house, and orbs have appeared in the photos. In one of the photographs, there is a ghostly boot, which looks like someone's leg has been cut off, rather than a picture of an empty boot, a docent said. She was unable to provide more information on why the boot in the photo looked more like an amputated leg, except that's what it seemed to look like, she said. Also, despite not being allowed to take photos, the ghost investigators have shown the pictures taken at Woodlawn Plantation to staff members on an unofficial basis, mostly to get the reaction of the staffers.

In addition, a psychic who walked through the premises reported "there's a feeling of something angry here," and the psychic then pointed to a portrait of Edward George Washington Butler, the Lewis' son-in-law, and said, "It's him." Mr. Butler was married to Frances Park, the Lewis' eldest daughter, but he was disliked by Major Lewis and Nelly, so the Butlers left Woodlawn for a sugar plantation outside of New Orleans. However, Butler's portrait still hangs at Woodlawn, where it frequently falls off the wall.

Reports by other staff members include candles lighting themselves after being blown out, and former Woodlawn employee Craig Tuminaro, who worked there several years, reported a strange occurrence his first year at the estate. Tuminaro was in the parlor, near the center hallway, when he "...heard a whisper." While Tuminaro described the sound as a whisper, he was not able to definitely identify what the whisper was trying to impart. It sounded like "swing" or "sweet" or "sshh," Tuminaro is reported to have said.

The Woodlawn Plantation

Chapter

5

Legends, Tall Tales, Tragedies and Nightmares

Introduction and Market Square

By American standards "Old Town" Alexandria is an old community. When the Old Town section was laid out, all the streets were nice and square, creating a very simple and regular configuration that focused on the waterfront. There was only one open area, or common public space, and that is Market Square. It is called Market Square because it is the oldest active market in the United States. Farmers still sell produce there on weekends, but is it known for other things as well. George Washington marched his troops in Market Square, and it still houses the court house—which at one time was the only civic building in Alexandria—and it included the sheriff, the jail cells, the judges, chambers, and all the records of the county hall being filed there, so a lot of important things happened at that location. It was also the place of punishment. There were no penitentiaries in the colonial era, so confinement was relatively short during this era—mostly until the accused went to trial. Corrections were mostly by fines, or by physical punishment.

Market Square in Old Town Alexandria.

One of the most common punishments of the colonial era was being locked into stocks for one to three days. Locking someone into stocks was the punishment for minor offenses such as stealing a loaf of bread, stealing fruit, or even riding your horse too fast. In addition to being locked on display as a lawbreaker, the towns' people could fling rotten fruits and vegetables at the offender with as much force as they could. In addition, all the men of the period carried walking sticks. The offender serving time in the stocks was bent over with no way to protect him or herself, so it was common for a gentleman to walk up to the prisoner from behind and give them a good smack across the backside as hard as he could. That was colonial era rehabilitation, for it was designed to keep minor offenders from entering into a life of crime.

Of course there was a whipping post, with flogging reserved for more serious infractions, and for capital crime, there was the rope. However, there were no permanent gallows in Alexandria. When there was a need for a hanging, a public executioner would be imported from Williamsburg, which was the colonial capital, and gallows would be built, leading up to the day of execution. Sometimes, all did not go as planned. Generally, a noose was placed around the condemned's neck and an open trap door would cause either near instant death from a broken neck, or a slow, painful death by strangulation.

One who probably got his just desserts, but who cheated the executioner at the same time, was an individual named "Kraven" or "Craven" Bowa, who was killed and is buried in the Presbyterian Graveyard. Mr. Bowa is America's first known serial murderer. His "modus operandi" was to hang out in a cabin in Alexandria and watch the ships dock. Specifically, he was watching for the sailors who would come into town looking to blow off some steam and have a good time before rejoining their ships. Bowa knew that sailors on liberty were carrying their wages when they came ashore, and in many cases they would get drunk. On dark nights, Bowa would follow sailors as they left the taverns. The seamen would be headed back to their ships, but some seamen never made it. However, one night Bowa met up with the wrong sailor, who was able to stick a knife into Bowa before Bowa could stick one into the seaman. Bowa had a belly wound, and he knew such a wound was fatal. So with only had a short time left, Bowa must have decided to leave this Earth with a clear conscious because, before he died, Bowa confessed to his crimes, saying he had murdered more men than he could remember. Following his confession, Bowa cheated the hangman, for he died of his wound.

Another criminal who avoided the hangman, but who nonetheless felt the wrath of Alexandria's righteous people, was Thomas McCoy. In the 1890s, Thomas McCoy was arrested and accused of kidnapping a girl named Annie Lacey. McCoy came to the attention of the police for the kidnapping of Annie Lacy because he had been seen stalking girls in their early teens. When questioned by the police commissioner, McCoy cracked, confessed, and told the police commissioner where her body was located, which was in the basement of McCoy's house. But in a stroke of good fortune for the girl, Annie Lacey still had a spark of life in her when the officials found her. When the nearly lifeless girl was returned to her family, the police commissioner was able to gage the mood of the crowd, and he knew there was a strong likelihood of trouble. So when he returned to Market Square, the commissioner assigned an extra security force to protect McCoy.

However, while McCoy would have gone to trial in less than a month for the kidnapping, rape, and near murder of Annie Lacey, the town's people wanted justice to be imposed sooner. Within a few hours a mob formed in the square and tried to break into the jail, but the extra security was able to keep them out. The commissioner believed the crowd would return with more vigilantes, so he had McCoy moved to the basement and hidden in a barrel. A few hours later, a mob consisting of hundreds of townsfolk laid siege to the jail, broke down the doors, and flooded in. The mob was able to relieve the guards of their weapons and searched the cells for McCoy. Not finding him in a cell, the crowd broke up and searched the rest of the jail, including the basement, where they found McCoy hiding in a barrel. He was dragged out of the jail and around the square to the southwest corner, where a large tree grew. They tied him to the tree, and six of the town's people formed an impromptu firing squad. They pulled out their weapons and simultaneously shot McCoy in the chest. Having administered "justice," the mob dispersed, and McCoy's body was allowed to remain in the square for a few days. However, once McCoy's body really started to decompose, it was taken to the Potomac River and dumped. While Thomas McCoy is dead, his legend, and possibly his spirit, lives on as a ghost stalking Market Square.

Another long-time favorite Market Square story involves a mean fellow named "Victor"—it's the only name known for him—who considered himself a ladies man. Victor lived sometime in the early colonial period and seemed in every sense to be a gentleman. He was well dressed and had enough money to be comfortable. The general belief is he was probably a "remittance man," an eighteenth century term for someone who is paid an allowance—a remittance—by his family to stay away. It was usually someone who was on the run from the law or who had created a scandal, so they would be sent somewhere else, and supplied with money under the condition he did not return.

Whatever Victor was, he cut a swath through the town's young women of the working class, mostly barmaids and domestic maids. Victor thought he was a skilled hand with the ladies, but unfortunately it was a right cross … he liked to hit women. Most of the women in the circles where Victor sought companionship were abused, but, Alexandria was still a small place back then, and when word got out about Victor, no one wanted anything to do with him. The story goes that on one afternoon Victor approached a woman in the town and made a request that she refused. He reacted by striking her, but when she went down she hit her head on a stone and died instantly. The crime occurred in front of several witnesses, so there was no question of his guilt. After a short trial, he was sentenced to hang. Eighteenth century executions were public entertainment, and the condemned was always given the chance to speak, (that's where the entertainment came from). What would he do?

Would the condemned announce a religious conversion, claim innocence, or be defiant. Victor was led out to the gallows, bowing to members of the crowd—which included young women he had abused—as he passed on his way to the gallows. Once he was securely placed on the gallows' trap door, Victor was asked if he would like to speak, and he said he would. Victor nodded to some of the women he had abused and said, "I'll be back." Victor could not have made a clearer threat to haunt those who were celebrating his demise.

The Ramsey House

William Ramsey immigrated to Virginia from Dumfrieshire, Scotland, and he did not land in Alexandria, but rather twenty-five miles to the south in what is now known as Dumfries. Like many other people, Mr. Ramsey was in the tobacco business, but for the tobacco to be exported to England, before leaving the colonies it had to pass through a King's inspection warehouse,

The Ramsey House at 221 North King Street, Alexandria is said to be haunted by Dennis Ramsey.

which was located in Alexandria. Because of that, Mr. Ramsey came to the conclusion that instead of having the tobacco collected in Dumfries and then shipped north to the inspection warehouse, why not set up operation where the warehouse was located?

In order to create tobacco facilities in Alexandria, Mr. Ramsey and Mr. Carlyle approached the Alexander family—because they owned the land—with the idea, and an agreement was reached. The next step involved getting approval from Virginia's House of Burgesses, which it did. Once that was complete, the Alexanders gave up forty-two acres of land to set up Alexandria as it is known today. Those forty-two acres were divided into half-acre lots, but the sale of those lots was made with the restriction that a house containing a brick chimney had to be built on the lot within a year, or the land reverted to the town. Mr. Ramsey purchased the land at 221 North King Street, and he was excited about owning property in the new town of Alexandria. However, the money he used to buy the land was all he had and he could not have a new home built on the land. Therefore, he had his home in Dumfries loaded onto a barge and transported to its present location, which was only possible because in the 1600s, the shore of the Potomac River ran right up to the back of the Ramsey house, which is now Alexandria's Visitor Center.

The house is haunted by either Mr. Ramsey himself, or his son, Dennis, who served as the mayor of Alexandria. Employees at the Visitors Center frequently say they hear footsteps going up and down the stairs, but when they look, there's no one there. The third floor is an office, and footsteps have been heard "stomping" around that floor, sounding as if someone is upset about something. This is why some ghost investigators believe it is Dennis, because he is reported to have fallen in love with a serving maid at a local tavern, but Mr. Ramsey put an end to any chances for a romance between the two, and they were successfully kept apart. Dennis never forgave his father for the rest of his life and the residue energy of that strong resentment Dennis had for his father could account for the haunting of the building.

The John Douglas Brown House

There is a theory that when some people die, they don't realize it, so their spirit will return to a location that was special to them. The John Douglas Brown House, located at 517 Prince Street, is likely such a place. The dwelling is also known as the Facet House because it remained in the Facet family from 1816 until 2000 when it was sold to the current owner. However, John Douglas Brown owned the home during the colonial era and while it was a small, unremarkable house, Mr. Brown would open it up to travelers who needed a place to stay for the night. During the Revolutionary War, Mr. Brown housed soldiers; however, he did more than house them. Mr. Brown tended the wounds of the injured, he fed them all, and he let them rest there until it was time for them to move on. Apparently some of the soldiers

The John Douglas Brown House at 517 Prince Street, Alexandria.

never forgot Mr. Brown's hospitality because several have been seen walking around on the grounds and inside the house. In the 1990s, the owner's grandchildren were spending the night at the house, and they were staying on the top floor. The children—a girl of twelve, a boy of nine—were sleeping and in the middle of the night the boy woke up to see what he is later reported to have described as a Revolutionary War soldier standing next to the bed where his sister slept. The boy was frightened and screamed, causing the ghost to vanish. Despite the boy's fright, no one believes the ghost meant any harm. Rather, it is likely the ghost was safeguarding the girl, much as he was safeguarded while under the care of Mr. Brown, more than two centuries earlier.

The Police Station Apparitions

At one point during the colonial era, the old Police Department was located on St. Asap Street. The St. Asap facility was not too big back then and the cells were located where the sergeants kept watch. The story says there were two inmates who had engaged in mostly petty crimes until they killed an elderly couple during a street robbery. This pair was quickly caught, tried, found guilty, and condemned to hang. They were then housed at St. Asap Station while awaiting execution.

As can be expected, both were terrified of hanging and they did not sleep well, moaning and cursing through the night. During the day they paced back and forth and their lack of sleep and pacing had the authorities concerned the two might attempt suicide in order to avoid hanging. So at night an officer was assigned to sit outside their cell. About two weeks before the scheduled execution, the officer outside the cell had fallen asleep. But he was awoken by a commotion, and saw the two inmates running down the corridor and up a flight of stairs. He yelled for help from another officer on duty who joined in the chase to recapture the fleeing prisoners. The officers both saw the two convicts turn a corner, but when the guards also turned the corner, the inmates were gone. At that point the two officers were convinced the inmates had escaped, taking the officers' law enforcement careers with them. They turned and were headed back to the desk to sound the alarm when they passed the cell where the condemned men were being housed. They looked in and the two men were still there sleeping. The officers had no idea what had happened.

Two days later, the second officer, who had assisted the first, was finishing a shift when he saw the same two figures that he had seen running through the station, again fleeing down a corridor and out the front door of the police station. The officer and desk sergeant took up chase, and when they got outside, they didn't find anyone. The sergeant immediately demanded to know how the two could have escaped and the officials ventured into the area where the cells were to find the officer who had been assigned to sit outside the condemned men's cell asleep. But the cell door was securely locked and both inmates were still in the jail. The sergeant entered the cell, shook one of the prisoners, and the man fell off the cot onto the floor. The prisoner was dead. The sergeant immediately checked the second prisoner and found he was dead too. Because the inmates died in custody, there was an investigation, but the cause of death could not be determined. The prisoners had just died, and no one was able to explain the specters that were seen running through the police station.

The police station apparitions is "a very strange story" that is "part of Alexandria's lore," said a ghost tour guide. Apparently, the prisoners were so terrified of facing judgment on the gallows, that they attempted escape the only way they knew how; that is they willed they spirits free from their earthly confinement.

The Voices in the Attic

In November of 1964, an old, run down house on Lee Street in Alexandria fell into the possession of a couple who had inherited it from the husband's uncle. Lee Street is named in honor of Confederate General Robert E. Lee, but its original name was Water Street because it is situated about a block from the Potomac River and frequently flooded (much of Old-Town Alexandria will flood today when heavy rains cause the Potomac to overflow).

In an effort to decide if they should sell the house, or have it repaired, the nephew and his wife went to the dwelling to inspect it. The house was completely empty, or so the couple thought.

The nephew and his wife entered the dwelling and started what was a fairly routine inspection of the property, but that soon changed because the couple heard voices. According to the couple, the voices sounded like a man and a woman, at times angry and arguing, and at other times it sounded as if someone was pleading, but they couldn't make out any words.

They believed that the real estate agent they had engaged had brought someone in to look at the house and had not told them, so they were hesitant to venture to that area of the house and possibly interrupt the sales pitch. However, they decided as the dwelling's owners, if they met the prospective buyers they might be able to answer some questions. So they looked for the visitors all through the house, but couldn't find anyone. They went up to the third—and top—floor and entered a bedroom but still couldn't find who was speaking. The couple did notice that the voices seemed to be coming from a closet. When they opened the closet the voices got louder, but still no one. At the back of the closet, they found there was a frame on the wall and the voices seemed to be coming from beyond the frame. The nephew reached for the frame, pulled it toward him and it came free, revealing a false wall, beyond which was a small room with a skylight. In the room were an old table and chair, and a pile of rags, and that was all. More importantly, the voices stopped and were never heard again. The couple then decided to have the house demolished and they sold the property to a developer.

Ten years later, totally by coincidence, the couple obtained a copy of a historical society journal which had a feature story about a letter written in 1864 by Confederate soldier Ezekiel Seay to his brother Meredith Seay, who was also a Confederate soldier. In the letter, Ezekiel wrote he had fallen ill, and his aliment caused him to become separated from his unit and eventually captured by a "Yankee cavalry patrol." The letter says Ezekiel was taken to Alexandria and admitted into a Union hospital, from which he escaped during the night. Once free from the hospital, Ezekiel said he wandered the streets until the sun started to rise, and in "fear and desperation" he knocked on the first door he saw at a house on Water Street (unfortunately Ezekiel did not include the house number). "By the best of luck, the lady inside was an ardent sympathizer because her husband had been killed in action at Second Manassas." Ezekiel also says she hid him "in a most secure and secret chamber." He also said the lady wanted him to stay because she did not believe him to be well enough to travel, but it was his intention "to attempt to leave the city as soon as the night is dark enough." Attached to the letter in the journal was a note that Ezekiel Seay was listed as having been in a Union hospital, escaped, and found frozen to death on Water Street.

After reading the letter, the couple became certain that the house mentioned in the missive was the house where they heard the voices. They also knew that the person who had owned the house before the uncle was a Quaker, and it is likely the house's safe room was used by Quakers—who were anti-slavery—as a stop on the Underground Railroad. The couple also believed that the voices they heard were the voices of Ezekiel Seay and the lady of the house.

The Pirates of Prince Street

Alexandria was a seaport at its inception, and it thrived as such through the Civil War when the Union used it to move men and supplies. During the colonial era, it was not unusual for 100 ships to be docked simultaneously on the Potomac River as they waited to head north to Georgetown and Baltimore, or south to Hampton Roads, or out to sea. Ships that docked in the Potomac at or near Alexandria carried not only cargo and passengers, but also their crews. Because the sailors' wages were low, the mariners were known to supplement their incomes by selling goods obtained in foreign ports that were difficult to come by in Alexandria. However, the problem colonial era smugglers faced was getting such loot off the ship and onto land without being seen by thousands of sailors. One of the ways the smugglers solved

Pirates once lived and died at 819 Prince Street, Alexandria.

that problem was by using an extensive network of tunnels that ran from the waterfront right into the basements of buildings.

There were two pirates who operated out of 819 Prince Street, Alexandria, and who likely used such tunnels to transport large chests of stolen tea, which they sold on the black market. However, while prosperous, the smuggling operation only lasted about two years.

It fell apart because jealousy and greed got the better of the pirates. After a successful run, the two buccaneers are known to have gotten into a shouting match, and one of the partners went missing.

Because the pirates were known to be partners, when one went missing, tongues wagged and there was speculation that the body was dumped at sea, or tossed into a fire pit outside of town. However, in 1903, the then resident of the house where the pirates had lived was awakened by the sound of pounding on a wall. It sounded as if it were coming from the basement, echoing through the entire house. The pounding forced the resident out of bed to search the house, and eventually the basement, and once there, the pounding would stop. The pounding noise occurred every night for three weeks, until the resident became convinced the house was haunted. At the end of the third week he headed for the basement and saw what could only be described as a ghostly hand sticking out of the wall. The hand then disappeared. After his initial shock, the resident went to the wall to get a closer look and saw that boards had come loose. He tore the loose boards away and discovered a pair of trousers that were knotted at the legs and tied at the top. Opening the rotting cloth, the curious homeowner recoiled in shock and disgust. Within them was a dismembered human skeleton stuffed into the pant legs as if it were a sack. By his own hand and long after death, the ill-fated smuggler and pirate resolved the mystery of his disappearance and revealed the place where his remains had been stashed.

The Nightmare House

Tour guides will tell crowds that 201 North Fairfax Street is one of the most feared haunted buildings in Alexandria, but there is little to support that statement other than stories. The building at that address was considered a place to be wary of because of the type of spirit activity there. While most ghosts are believed to approach when the living are awake and able to see them, the ghosts at 201 North Fairfax Street, however, come to those who are sleeping and they only haunt the living in their dreams. In 1777, the building's owner rented out the basement apartment

The Nightmare House at 201 North Fairfax Street, Alexandria. A historical marker is on the left.

to a dentist who lived and set up shop in that basement apartment, and is the first recorded victim of the dream hauntings. The dentist occupied the dwelling for a few years; then he suddenly disappeared. No one knows what happened to him.

Today, 201 North Fairfax Street is an office building, which is fortunate, as it is difficult for sensitive people to spend the night there, or so the lore suggests. The nightmares are awful. However, before it became known as Alexandria's haunted terror, the building was originally "Wise's Tavern." Another of George Washington's "haunts," and it is known for being the place where he was first called "President." There is even a historical marker, which reads:

> Wise's Tavern
> 1788-1792
> Here on April 16, 1789 George Washington was for the first time publicly addressed as President of the United States.

After the building stopped being Wise's Tavern, the dwelling became a boarding house, and remained so through the Great Depression. There are at least two different versions of the nightmare, but there's no way to tell which of the versions of the story is the original, or if these versions have any resemblance to what really happened.

The Fire Nightmare

One version of the story focuses on two women who lived in the boarding house during the Depression and who were doing their laundry. As they were doing their chores, one of the ladies tells her companion that she has been having the "craziest dreams" for the past couple of weeks. "I've been having the same dream every night."

Her friend asks, "What kind of dream are you having?"

The first woman says, every night in my dream, "I sit up in bed and I'm absolutely terrified. For some reason I know I'm going to die because the building is on fire and the roof is going to cave in on top of me." At that point she would wake up petrified, her heart racing madly.

Of course, the second woman reassures the first woman that it is only a dream. Nothing to get excited about, she's just imagining everything. But, the story goes, one-by-one the building's tenants all begin to have the same dream. Still nothing happened. There was no fire, the roof didn't cave in, and life went on. Eventually, the building was sold again, and it was converted from a boarding house into a home for the elderly. However, once the elderly tenants were moved into the building, they started complaining about dreaming the building was on fire and the roof was caving in, killing the dreamers. However, just as with the boarding house tenants, the building did not catch fire and the roof did not collapse.

It was later discovered that when the building was under construction, it did catch fire. Workmen were trapped on the third floor … when the roof caved in, killing them all.

The Pit Nightmare

The other version of this story begins with the original owner, after a respectable amount of time following the dentists' disappearance, again renting out the apartment, and subsequent owners have done this for more than 200 years. But, each tenant reported enduring three different recurring nightmares. The first nightmare has the tenant hanging on for dear life over a dark, bottomless pit. The second nightmare is a variation of the fire dream; the building is on fire and the walls and building are caving in on the sleeping tenant. The third nightmare is enough to drive people out of the room. It usually occurs from 5 a.m. to 6 a.m. when the tenant is nearly awake but not quite, almost as if they were hypnotized. The sleeping tenant dreams that he or she is in their room sleeping with someone sitting in a chair by the bed. The dreamers have described the unwanted visitor as an older, roughly middle-aged man, sitting in a rocking chair. He's rocking back and forth, with a knife plunged into his right eye. One of the tenants who had this dream decided just talking about it wasn't enough. He believed a member of the spirit world was attempting to communicate with the sleeper in the room, so he did some research and found that many colonial homes have a dry well—a deep pit under the house—to dispose of garbage. The man reasoned that since the building dated back to the colonial era, there was a good chance it had a dry well, and if he was able to examine the well, it might provide some clues to the nightmares. He began to examine the floorboards of his basement apartment, and after a period of investigation, he found the building's dry well.

He pulled up the floorboards and found the well to be covered over with boards. These aging boards were easy to remove and once he gained access, he found the well went down about nine feet. At the bottom of the well he found colonial artifacts, broken teacups, pieces of pottery, things that a colonial family would use on a daily basis. The man reached the conclusion that it had to be connected to the first nightmare—hanging by your fingertips over a dark pit. Obviously that was the pit, and those were the objects on the bottom. That accounted for the first nightmare, so his attention turns to the second. He searched the room looking for something that might explain the nightmares when he found a plank of wood that was burned black on one side. He concluded that the nightmare was focused on the building catching fire at least once, and being rebuilt. The man's attention is said to have focused on the third nightmare, and he descended into the dry well again. He continued to search through the pile of garbage and he found human remains among the refuse, with a knife embedded into the right eye. While the skeleton has not been established to be the remains of the missing dentist, there have been no more reports of nightmares since its discovery. Exactly what caused some of the building's occupants to experience unpleasant dreams is not known, but while the nightmares experienced at the building seem to be at an end, the building's reputation remains, leaving a stigma on the structure to the point of urban legend.

Chapter

6

The Carlyle House

Scottish merchant John Carlyle—who in 1749 was one of the three families that founded Alexandria—oversaw the completion of his mansion in 1753. The house, located at 121 North Fairfax Street, was for his bride, Sarah Fairfax of Belvoir, Virginia. Sarah was from one of the most prestigious families in colonial Virginia. Her cousin was Lord Thomas Fairfax, who owned more than 5.28 million acres of Virginia and who Fairfax County is named for. While Mr. Carlyle obviously sought to increase his social standing by marrying into such a grand family, he did not know that in 1755 his home—which by then had become a center of social life for Alexandria's gentry—would be at the center of events that would change the world.

Mr. Carlyle had the home designed in the Georgian Palladian style, and indentured servants and slave labor began work on the house in 1751. Ever mindful of his standing in

The Carlyle House, located at 121 North Fairfax Street, Alexandria, is said to be haunted by John Carlyle's second wife, Syble.

The Carlyle House

the community, Mr. Carlyle had the home built with public and private concerns in mind, ensuring there were both public spaces for entertaining and private areas for family and servants. Mr. Carlyle also arranged the surrounding dependencies and landscaping according to the needs of both his household and his business. The outbuildings serviced both the family lifestyle (necessary, smokehouse, etc.) and his merchant business (office, warehouses). Although construction took almost three years, Carlyle's completed home signified both his status as a gentleman and his business enterprises.

Roots of Revolution

In the years prior to the American Revolution, Alexandria was one of the principal colonial trading centers and ports. During this era, England and France fought over land claims in the trans-Allegheny region, which is known in colonial history as the French and Indian War. That conflict occurred in what was "British North America" and was considered to be an extension of the wars in Europe, therefore King George III sent General Edward Braddock to lead the attack on the French and their Indian allies.

Upon his arrival in Alexandria with 1,200 British troops, General Braddock selected Carlyle's house as his headquarters and the general, along with his aides, took residence in the home for three weeks. While pondering the military situation, on April 14, 1755, Braddock also convened a meeting with five royal governors of the colonies, but at the meeting the general did more than inform the governors of his plans for the coming campaign. During the meeting, Braddock discussed ways to fund the campaigns and he said it would be necessary to tax all his Majesty's dominions in America. That was the beginning of colonial resentment against England. Soon, cries of "taxation without representation" were heard and would eventually rally the colonists against the crown. However, that was yet to come, and on April 15, 1755, John Carlyle wrote to his brother George of the meeting. John's pride that his house was selected beamed through the letter which said, "There was the grandest congress held at my home ever known on the continent."

But it would not take very long for Carlyle to become disillusioned with Braddock, who helped increase colonists' resentment for him by not bothering to hide his contempt for the local residents. Carlyle later wrote to his brother George that General Braddock was a man "too fond of his passions, women, and wine..." and that while in his home the general had "abused my house and furnishings..." Carlyle was happy to see Braddock leave on the campaign from which the general would not return. However, the wheels of rebellion had started to move and as a direct result of the meeting of royal governors, such local leaders as George Washington and George Mason met on July 18, 1774, at Alexandria's courthouse, where Mason's "Fairfax Resolves"—calling for an end to trade with England—were adopted. The courthouse is directly across the street from the Carlyle house where the seeds of revolution were planted more than nineteen years before.

While it is amazing that the Carlyle house played such a pivotal role in U.S. history, the history of the house and its ghostly inhabitants also intrigues many. John Carlyle was born into a wealthy family, but because he was not the oldest son, he was denied the family fortune. Therefore, he traveled to Virginia representing a tobacco merchant, a line of work that he turned out to be very good at. He was so good that he was able to build his huge home, which he sought to protect from ghosts and bad luck by interring the remains of a cat within its walls. If the cat's remains were to ward off bad luck, it didn't work out so well for Mr. Carlyle, for both of his wives, and thirteen of his fourteen children died at the home, and a good number of his slaves also died on the property.

Of the two wives who died at the Carlyle house, it is believed the building is haunted by Mr. Carlyle's second wife, Syble West, daughter of prominent Alexandrian Hugh West. Syble was so jealous of John's late first wife Sarah that Syble had all of Sarah's possessions burned in a bonfire. In addition,

Syble issued an edict to the servants and slaves saying she was now the mistress of the house and any of them who referred to Sarah as the mistress would be severely punished (whipping may have been mentioned, but there is no real proof of that). Because Syble's jealous rage was legendary, it is also believed that her anger can be used to provoke her into making an appearance, or at least to making her ghostly presence known. To do that, legend says, have a woman, or girl, whose name is Sarah, knock on the front door while others say, "Sarah, come outside!" While an amusing custom, there haven't been any reports of ghostly appearances as a result of that practice.

John Carlyle died in 1780, and upon his death, his oldest daughter, Sarah, lived in the house with her family. However, by 1827 the Carlyle family had lost possession of the house, and for the next fifty years it passed through many hands. During that period, the property served a variety of purposes, including as a Civil War hospital, a hotel, and a private residence. In 1970, the Northern Virginia Regional Park Authority acquired the property, and after six years of restoration, the house and gardens were opened to the public as a museum.

According to Alexandrians, while Syble is the most well known Carlyle House ghost, she is not the only spirit active at the dwelling. After the Carlyle family lost possession of the house, the buildings on both sides were purchased by a Mr. James Green who opened up a hotel—the Mansion House Hotel—which had the reputation as one of the finest hotels on the East Coast. To make the best use of the space, Mr. Green had a bridge built connecting the structures and there are still indentations in the building next door to the mansion which mark the spots where wood beams were shoved into the bricks to support the bridge, from which at least three fell to their deaths. The spirits of those unfortunate individuals are also said to be haunting the house.

However, despite stories of Syble's jealous ghost, there are conflicting opinions as to whether there are any ghostly activities, and if there are of what type, occurring at Carlyle House. Local tour guides say that when photos of the front

The Washington DC Metro Area Ghost Watchers (DCMAG) was founded in 2002 by Al Tyas, a federal employee with a strong interest in the paranormal. Mr. Tyas ran DCMAG for five years, at which point he left the group to pursue other, similar interests. The current head of DCMAG is John Warfield, who is retired from the U.S. military, and has spent much of his time putting together a new team to conduct investigations into alleged haunting in the District of Columbia, Southern Maryland, Northern Virginia and beyond the Beltway.

About 120 investigations were conducted when Mr. Tyas ran the group, Mr. Warfield said. "Since I've been on board, I've done about fifteen investigations, and I'm trying to expand the team; we're at ten members right now, that are split up into two teams, allowing them to do investigations every other week," he added. There are certain times of the year, which Mr. Warfield considers DCMAG's "busy season," and Halloween is one of those times. During the autumn and around Halloween, people believe their houses are haunted, and those investigations help increase the group's profile around the community. "I want to make the group known to the greater Washington, D.C. community, and let the public know we're not a bunch of people running around wearing heavy-metal T-shirts, stomping around graveyards; that we actually care about the community. We want to help them and educate them about paranormal experiences. We have a good group of people who are very professional," he said. Warfield stresses to the team not to show up at a site or a graveyard and "stomp around." It is not ethical to operate that way, he said. "I try to tell people, someday we're all going to be dead, and we'll have to answer to these people when we die."

The group so far includes retired and active duty police officers, retired military, and others who hold stable, ordinary jobs, and the more stable looking the person is, the more likely DCMAG will welcome them into their ranks. "When the group is recruiting, we look for professionalism, and if they have a good heart. When we find someone with those qualities, you can teach them everything else," Mr. Warfield said. DCMAG recruits the same way any other company recruits candidates, he added. "I am contacted by people who want to join the group, who say they are professional, and they'll provide me with an e-mail address saying 'deathangel666@' or something like it," he said. Those people usually get a thank you, but are never contacted again because it is clear that they are not at all professional, he added.

A Scent of Roses

Jan Cunard is from Prince William County, Virginia, and she is an active volunteer involved with different groups including historic preservation, and that helped her find DCMAG, she said. "I've been interested in the supernatural since high school. I wrote a paper on poltergeists," she said. However, it was not until she was an adult and involved with paranormal events that she took a real interest in ghost investigation, Ms. Cunard said. The first incident occurred at her home. It was during the winter, but the unmistakable scent of roses filled her house. Because of the season, there weren't any roses in bloom anywhere near the house, but the scent was there and it created a great sense of calm, peacefulness, and seemed to say "everything is going to be okay," she said. That first incident made her a believer.

The first experience with the fragrance of roses seemed to have opened lines of communication with Ms. Cunard, because the scent of roses would follow her around the country, including on a trip to Minnesota to see her mother who was gravely ill and near death. "Her kidneys were shutting down, and all the signs were that she was not going to make it. My brother and I spent the day with her and she was given the last rites," she said. Ms. Cunard eventually had to leave the hospital to start the funeral arrangements. The next morning was a Sunday—it was late November and it was the Sunday before Thanksgiving—and while she wanted to return to the hospital, her brother urged her to go to church with him and pray, and have everyone in church pray for their mother, she said. After church her brother convinced her that they needed to have breakfast before returning to the hospital. The hospital cafeteria was closed on Sundays—it's a small town with a small hospital—so the siblings stopped at a people. When an individual does contact the group, Warfield will conduct a phone interview "to make sure they are on the up," he said. If, after the phone interview, the decision is made to proceed, a walk through the house is conducted to give the group an "idea of the house and what obstacles" the group might have to face. "Also, to once again make sure they are legitimate," he said. If the group believes further action is necessary, then it's up to the client to decide to go further or not. And by further action, that might mean just a phone consultation where the client is given advice on what to do, or they might conduct a full investigation, he said.

If the decision is made to conduct a full investigation, the group hopes to gather EVP, but if there are apparitions the members will concentrate on photography. But the first thing the team does at an investigation is establish a baseline of the home's electromagnetic field (EMF) frequency, Mr. Warfield said. By establishing the houses' baseline EMF frequency they can determine what the energy levels are in the dwelling so that if deviations from the baseline EMF show up on the equipment and monitors, the group will be ready. As some members of the group wait and watch their monitors, two teams will go through the house monitoring for EVP.

The majority of that work is conducted at night, because most experiences involving ghosts occur at night, Mr. Warfield said. If an experience occurs during the day, the group would investigate during the day, but group members have never had that experience. Once the equipment is set up, the group monitors for movement. "At one site we saw curtains move, and we ran to that room and found a vent right underneath the curtain. However, the cameras also record sound, and at another investigation a camera picked up some EVP. It was the sound of a ghost calling a member of the team a 'whore'," Mr. Warfield said.

The incident in which an EVP voice is heard saying the word "whore" occurred at a Civil War era jail in Brentsville, Virginia. The jail building, which is no longer a working jail, is owned by the Brentsville Courthouse Historic Centre and DCMAG was conducting the investigation with the historical centre's permission. Ms Cunard said the group was asking questions and "got responses immediately after asking, which indicates that it is an intelligent haunting, rather than a residual."

On the tape of the incident, a group member is heard asking, "Have you ever met James Clark before?" (James Clark was killed in the jail by the angry brother of a woman Clark was accused of "leading astray.") The EVP response is, "Get out," but it is quiet, almost a whisper. In contrast, the word "Whore" is loud and unmistakable. Mr. Warfield believes the spirit was calling a member of the group a whore. "We were getting high EMF readings as that happened. We knew something was going on, but then that," he said. The EVP has been posted on DCMAG's web site and is available for listening by anyone. "We'll present it as is, and some people are going to believe there's a ghost there, and others won't," he said.

The Brentsville Jail is not the only investigation DCMAG has conducted in Prince William County, Virginia. In Dumfries, the group also conducted an investigation at a building of historical significance called the Williams Ordinary. During the colonial era, an "ordinary" was an establishment that provided travelers with an ordinary meal and sleeping space. Such places were also called taverns or inns. Williams Ordinary is believed to have been built in the 1760s, although the exact construction date is unknown. The building's symmetrical facade features a brick pattern known as header bond, a pattern that is rarely found in Virginia. This building was one of the most prominent structures in colonial Dumfries and reflected the port town's importance and wealth. While the building is known as Williams Ordinary, records are unclear as to whether local tavern keeper George Williams occupied this structure during the 1700s. Research on the building is ongoing, but it is known the building's name has changed to indicate various owners or uses. It has been called Love's Hotel, Old Love's Tavern, the Brick Tavern, and the Stagecoach Inn.

DCMAG conducted its investigation at Williams Ordinary not long after the county acquired the property, Ms Cunard said. What really attracted the group to conduct an investigation was the previous owner's descriptions of several strange incidents, including one night when his family woke up and found that all the clocks—electric and battery operated—had stopped at 2 a.m. So the group decided to focus on 2 a.m. as part of the investigation, and the night of the investigation the group hit a time distortion. Just before 1 a.m. on the night of the investigation, the county official in charge of the building showed up at Williams Ordinary to sit with the group, Ms. Cunard said. We know it was just before 1 a.m. because as he was saying how anxious he was to see what happens at 2 o'clock, he received a page from his office. After he responded to the page, he was free to sit and watch the group investigate. The official and the group were making small talk when someone said, "Have you looked at your watches?" It was 2:45 in the morning. "Everyone's watch said 2:45 a.m. and none of us can explain the lost time," she said.

"I noticed it first," Mr Warfield said. "Because at 1:45 a.m. I was getting ready for an EVP session right at 2. Only about 15 minutes later I checked my watch and it said 2:45 a.m.," he said. He then asked the group if they realized what time it was. They replied, it's probably about 2 a.m. "I said, no it's almost 3 a.m.," Mr. Warfield said. They all said it couldn't be, and that's when everyone looked at their watches, and everyone realized that it was 2:45 a.m.

Dangerous Spirits

The group is perplexed by how the lost time could have occurred, and were concerned about the incident. Nonetheless, they did not feel they were in danger, and continued with the investigation. However, some of the hauntings can be dangerous, Mr. Warfield added. The level of danger depends on why a spirit or spirits remain at a location. Some spirits stay because they don't know they are dead, or they have unfinished business, or they are afraid of being judged by God; others just don't want to leave, and many of the hauntings involve ghosts who don't want to leave because they are attached to a place where they spent their whole lives. After they die, someone moves in and they get angry. It might not necessarily be that it's dangerous, but that the ghost doesn't want new people there, so there's activity to scare them away. In these cases there's usually an angry spirit, but no real danger. The cases involving real threats are demonic cases, he added. "I've been made aware of a couple of possible demonic cases, but I've never been able to follow through because the people were so afraid they didn't want us out there. Every time they tried to bring us out, the activity would increase, and they were afraid to call us back." One lady had an iron thrown at her head. There's one case where a gas stove was being turned on, and pillows in the house are being stacked up with remote controls on top to form an arrow. The people who lived there believed they were being ordered out of the house," he said.

A demonic haunting is an intelligent haunting, and demonic hauntings are very aggressive and very powerful, Mr. Warfield said. When such an entity is present in a house, the people living there will know it because there are signs such as growling noises, bad odors, and objects flying around the house. "It will be extremely aggressive to the point that it will let you know it is there if it wants to but it will also go into hiding if the people call for help," he said. The truth of the matter is that in many cases a demonic entity is somehow invited into the home, he added. People will play with Ouija boards. I try to tell people to never play with a Ouija board because it only allows in bad things, especially when someone doesn't know what they are doing, he said. A demonic spirit will disguise itself as the person's late grandmother to gain access to the house, and once in the home it can't be easily gotten rid of, he said. In addition, in most demonic hauntings there's usually more of a problem than just someone using an Ouija board, he added. Demonic entities are usually attracted to a lot of negativity, he said. Those entities will revolve around alcoholics, drug abusers, child molesters, or people who physically abuse their families, to list a few. The demonic entity craves those environments, and attempts to change that environment will cause such entities to react with anger. Many times when members of the group conduct an initial visit, they won't find anything because the entity does not want them to know it is there. However, clients have reported that the activity got worse after the initial visit, and, because of that, some clients don't want us to come back. "I tell them it is going to get worse before it gets better," he said. I'll then ask if I can bring in an "inhuman haunting specialist" (same thing as a demonologist) to do a house clearing. "But I tell them there's a chance it will or will not work," he said. I also tell them they need to take some initiative to clear up the issues such as alcohol and drug abuse that attracted this thing, and that it's not going to go away until they undertake some initiative to get rid of it, he said.

Belief

Despite their experiences, both with investigations and individually, members of DCMAG are not going to try and change anyone's belief on the subject of ghosts. "We don't know what all the evidence means. So we try and collect evidence in a way so that it's pure and unbiased. But people who are taking the evidence and adding it up and saying it means this, I think they are full of themselves because we're simply not there yet," Mr. Warfield said.

DCMAG member Dawn Boutelle said she doesn't believe there will ever be "a Holy Grail of evidence" that will convince people that spirits exist. "I think it's going to take many years of constant, consistent evidence for people to start to believe," she said. "But there are people who believe that the Holocaust in World War II didn't happen, so there are always going to be people who doubt, no matter how much evidence you have," she added.

Because many people are not ready to accept that ghosts exist, Mr. Rossi has "removed" himself from "trying to convince anyone of anything. I just present things and you'll add it up any way you want."

Chapter

8

The Merchant Family and
the Weems-Botts House

Located on Quantico Creek, the roots of Dumfries, Virginia, can be traced to 1690 when Richard Gibson erected a gristmill on that creek. A customhouse and warehouse followed in 1731, and many others cropped up along the estuary by 1732. Eventually, Prince William County was formed, taking its name from Prince William Augustus, the second son of King George II of England.

Then, Virginia's General Assembly established Dumfries as the first of seven townships in the county. The Town of Dumfries received its charter on May 11, 1749, and it was established on 60 acres of land provided by John Graham, at which a deepwater harbor was established on Quantico Creek. Mr. Graham named the new town after his birthplace of Dumfries, Scotland.

It was the port that made Dumfries special, said Weems-Botts Museum docent Emma Young. At one time Dumfries rivaled

One of the oldest buildings in Virginia, the Weems-Botts house, located at 3944 Cameron Street, Dumfries, is home to at least two ghosts.

The Merchant Family and the Weems-Botts House

Boston, New York, and Philadelphia as a major colonial port, and, much the same as the gentry in those cities, Virginia's most prominent families—including the Washingtons, the Masons, and the Lees—traveled to Dumfries to shop, eat, attend the theater or watch the horse races at its two race tracks. In addition, because the harbors in both Boston and New York had been under siege during the American Revolution, General Washington depended heavily on Dumfries for supplies, and he constantly worried the British would lay siege to the port, she said.

As Dumfries is one of oldest continuously chartered towns in Virginia, part of the Weems-Botts house—located at 3944 Cameron Street—is also one of the oldest buildings in Virginia, Ms. Young said. While the exact year of its construction is not known, records show that it was standing at its location by 1750, and while the building has housed individuals, it has nearly always doubled as a business, especially in its early years, she adds.

The current museum housed in the structure is named after the Reverend Mason Locke Weems and the man who purchased the house from Weems in 1802, Benjamin Botts, both of whom played special rolls in American history, Ms. Young said.

When Reverend Weems owned the house, he used it as a bookstore to sell copies of a "biography" of President Washington that was first published in 1800 and which included the anecdotes about Washington as a youth barking—removing the bark from—his father's cherry tree (which featured the famous "I cannot tell a lie" quote that Washington never said) as well as Washington throwing a stone across the Rappahannock River. In its time, the book was a best seller, second only to the Bible, and it remained in publication until 1927. The stories further established George Washington's legend for all time.

Benjamin Botts was a lawyer who used the house as his law office. Mr. Botts is most notable as a member of the legal team that in 1807 successfully defended former U.S. Vice President Aaron Burr against charges of treason. Tragically, in 1811, Mr. Botts and his wife Jane were killed in a theater fire in Richmond.

Ownership of the property changed hands several times until 1869 when the Merchant family—Richard, his wife Annie—gained possession of the dwelling. The Merchants', who had two boys when they moved in, and later two girls, were well established in Dumfries as early as the 1780s, and the family retained ownership of the house until 1968. The tragedies that befell the Merchant family are linked to the strange occurrences at the house.

Not long after the Merchants moved into the dwelling, the two boys died of tuberculosis early in their lives. Richard and Annie were left with daughters, Mamie and Violet. Sadly, Mamie was afflicted with epilepsy and suffered seizures. That caused the Merchants to turn to the Bible for guidance paying particular attention to the passages detailing those who exhibited similar symptoms, and came to believe that the ailment Mamie suffered from was not epilepsy, but demonic possession. Once the Merchants became convinced Mamie was possessed, she was taken to a bedroom on the second floor and locked away for the rest of her life. She literally did not leave that room. She was fed up there, she didn't even leave to go to the outhouse, rather, she was provided with a chamber pot, and the only human interaction she had was with her immediate family. In 1906, she died in the room at age twenty-three. Within months of Mamie's death, Richard died, and it's said he succumbed to a broken heart.

In the meantime, the Merchant's other daughter, Violet, had graduated from business college and moved to Washington, D.C. where she made a life for herself as a federal employee. At the time, most women of Violet's stature did not work. They lived with their families until they married, and certainly they only worked if they needed to. Violet did not need to work, but she joined the federal workforce nonetheless. Remember, there weren't any equal employment laws, and Violet's job application included a section in which the "attractiveness" of the applicant is rated. If an applicant did not get high enough attractiveness numbers, she would never get a job. Violet was rated "97" out of 100 points. In addition, Violet was engaged. However, when Richard died, Annie directed Violet to break off the engagement and return to Dumfries where she was to take care of her mother. Violet obliged and apparently lived with her mother until Annie died at ninety-nine years of age in 1954. Violet never got another job, or spent time with a man ever again. Rather, she spent the rest of her days in solitude and died thirteen years later in 1967. That is the end of the Merchant family. Five family members— two sons, Mamie, Richard, and Annie—died in the house. Violet left the house about two months before her death.

Conversion to a Museum

The Town of Dumfries acquired the property in 1969 and eventually converted the building into the Weems-Botts Museum. The museum covers the history of Dumfries, by having different rooms focus on different eras (Colonial, Federalist and Victorian). In 1974, as reparations were underway at the house in anticipation of it becoming a museum, strange occurrences began. The room where Mamie lived and died is reported to be extremely active with ghosts. Voices—including that of a little girl—have been heard in the room. Numerous psychics have conducted investigations of the house, and they have been amazingly accurate in the information provided on the Merchants.

The museum used to have a photograph of what they thought was Richard Merchant hanging in what is known as the "Victorian era room." But it was common to find the photo on a chair that was placed immediately under it, or on the floor. "It looked like someone threw it," Ms. Young said. "We use to think that one of the ghosts was mad at Richard for some reason, but we couldn't figure it out. But in 2008 the museum had the pictures of the Merchant family framed under 'museum glass,' which protects the photos from UV, and when they were removed from the frame, we found out it's not Richard, but it was William Alfred Speake, brother to Annie Merchant. So now we think they were trying to tell us, this isn't Richard."

There have been recent sightings of Violet and Mamie in the upstairs bedroom, Ms. Young said. In addition, in July 2008, the first sighting of Annie was reported, causing a stir among the museum's staff. The circumstances surrounding the sighting of Annie occurred on a Saturday, when the museum closes at 4 p.m. and remains closed until Tuesday. Annie was seen on Saturday, after closing hours, by a woman who did not know anything about the ghosts, or stories of the Merchant family, Ms. Young said. The woman called on Tuesday and said, "I tried to get the attention of your docent Saturday evening, but she wasn't paying any attention to me."

The first question the staff had was, are you sure it was Saturday evening? The woman said yes, adding she wanted to obtain information on the museum—pamphlets and such—and she was standing out on the street in front of the house when she noticed a "docent" in nineteenth century period costume standing in a window. She described what the woman in the window was wearing as a high-waisted skirt, with a white long-sleeve blouse that had a high collar. The woman said she waved in order to get the unidentified "docent's" attention, but the woman in period dress did not acknowledge the visitor's attempt to draw attention. Then the docent stepped away from the window. However, the woman could see that the docent moved to another part of the house, and she tried again to get her attention. But nothing worked, and the woman was miffed by the rude docent. The staff then showed her photos of the Merchant family, and the woman pointed to Annie and said, "That's her, that's the one I saw in the window."

The staff responded by saying, "You mean, this woman who died in 1954?"

The woman said, "What! That can't be right, that's the woman I saw!"

Mamie's Room

Objects move in Mamie's room, and closets just open, said Ms. Young, who added that she is "conducting an experiment." Before she leaves every night she ensures the closets are locked, and she has found them open in the morning.

Curtains are often opened, and local people have reported seeing someone in the upstairs room, but they could not provide details. But now there's the account identifying the person in the window as Annie.

Mamie Merchant's room: Mamie is most often seen in a corner of the room near the closet.

Mamie is most often seen in a corner of the small room near a closet, Ms. Young said, adding she was present when a psychic visited. The psychic went right for the corner, and not long after entering Mamie's room, the psychic said, "There's a mother here," according to Young. "He said he felt 'a strong mother presence', and it was only a few weeks after Annie was first sighted, Young added.

However, the most famous sighting in Mamie's room did not involve psychics. Rather, the sighting occurred while a group was touring the house, Young said. A Boy Scout troop from the Marine Base at Quantico, Virginia, was visiting, and a group of the Boy Scouts had just been shepherded into the room, including their scoutmaster. The scoutmaster was the last one up the steps—which lead directly into the room—and the leader was standing on the steps looking through the banister bars, and the docent who was leading the tour later described the scoutmaster as seeming to be physically agitated while standing on the steps. Nonetheless, the docent continued with the tour, talking about the room's furnishings and how people lived in the late 1800s, when the scoutmaster interrupted the tour. He was looking at the corner when he forcefully said, "Why don't you get her a chair." He sounded upset, but the docent did not understand what he was talking about. Finally, the docent said, "I don't know what you're talking about."

"She clearly wants her chair. Why don't you get her a chair?!" the scoutmaster responded.

"There's no one there," the docent replied. The blood drained from the scoutmaster's face and he is described as turning "white." He literally ran out of the house, and that frightened the Boy Scouts who ran out of the house right behind him, she said. Outside, the scoutmaster calmed down enough to describe a woman standing in the corner. He described her as a young woman dressed in dark clothing, and she was crying. He said she'd asked for her chair. The living Mamie is known to have had a rocking chair that she sat in quite often. That is the most famous sighting because the scoutmaster was a Marine who was not interested in ghost hunting—in fact he was a skeptic—and who wasn't easily frightened, but his experience sent him running out of the house, Ms. Young said.

There's a much less well known story involving ghost hunters who placed a video camera and tape recorder on the bed in Mamie's room and went downstairs to retrieve more equipment, Ms. Young said. When the ghost hunters returned, they found the camera and tape recorder were still on the bed, but they were each standing on a point. Both ghost hunters were astonished by what they saw, but one elbowed the other, causing the second ghost hunter to say, "I see it!" That caused the equipment to drop. But of course it was not captured on tape. They did record orbs flying about the room. They also made an electronic voice phenomenon (EVP) recording, but it sounds too distorted to fully understand anything, Ms. Young said. Nonetheless, there are unusual sounds on the tape that resemble conversation, and those sounds are not made by the people who were in the room, because you can clearly hear them asking if there is anyone present in the room as the recording is being made, she said.

The Merchant Family and the Weems-Botts House

The Colonial Room

In the Colonial room, which is a bedroom, there are two windows opposite each other, and Ms. Young believes that if both windows are open, a breeze would blow through the room. "It's kind of stuffy up there," said Ms. Young, who recounted the ghostly experience she had in that room. She was leading a tour and was gesturing to the small window, when she said, "You could open this window." At that instant, the window—which opens like a door and not up and down—opened as if it were thrown open. A woman on the tour commented on how the window opened when Ms. Young said, "Open."

"I said, 'Yes, that is strange, but who knows what's in the realm of possibility," the docent says. Ms. Young then used the opportunity to mention the house's ghost history. "And I jokingly said, 'maybe we could ask the ghost to close the window.' When I said 'close', bam, it shut." I was standing by the bed, and when the window slammed shut, I reacted by taking a step back.

The visiting woman's voice suddenly went up an octave to high pitch and she said, "It closed itself!" A man on the tour said, "That's so cool!"

"I'm a scientist by training, so I tend to look at things logically," said Ms. Young, who has degrees in Natural Resource Science and Environmental Sociology. Because the building is actually a museum, "In every room in the house there is a hidden temperature and humidity gauge, so I went and checked that. They were the same temperature and humidity as that morning. They hadn't changed, so I said to the group, 'we had a little ghost experience'." Ms. Young then continued with the tour, and started telling the group about a trunk from the colonial era that she likes because it is lined with deerskin. "I went on with the tour because you just don't see deer skin that much," she said. "So I gestured to the trunk and started to speak, when the window starts opening and closing nonstop and incredibly fast. It's open and shut, open and shut, open and shut, slamming. And as that's happening, I'm pretending to talk to the group about the trunk. And this goes on and on. I honestly don't know how long it went on for, but it went on for a long time. The whole time the tour group is starring at the window, and after a while I realize we'll go on watching this window open and close all day. I remembered that some psychics have said 'Violet is upset, because she's not discussed on the tours as much as the other members of the family.' So I said, 'Violet, I know you want me to talk about you, I promise I'll talk about you, but on the Victorian side. In the Colonial part of the building, I'm going to talk about Colonial history. When we go to the Victorian side, I will tell your story, but right now I need you to stop messing…' When I said 'stop', bam, the window slammed shut. It opened as soon as I said 'open'. It closed as soon as I said 'close'. And as soon as I used the word 'stop', it stopped. I have no other explanation for it. Nothing else in the room moved. It wasn't like during an earthquake where the whole building would shake. The only thing that was moving was that window. I have no physical explanation for that, other than something I couldn't see was doing that."

The Colonial Room has a window—directly behind the bed—that has been known to continuously open and slam shut.

Chapter

9

Sex and Death
in Occoquan

The Occoquan Inn, located at 301 Mill Street, Occoquan, Virginia.

The story of the haunting at the Occoquan Inn, located at 301 Mill Street, Occoquan, Virginia—a small town about twenty miles south of Alexandria—is a story of love, sex, and revenge, but unfortunately because the events related to the haunting at the inn occurred more than 250 years ago, details are difficult to come by. The roots of Occoquan began in 1734 when Virginia's General Assembly directed for the construction of a tobacco warehouse and trading post on the Occoquan River, and just as communities will grow around an industry or anchor business, it was no different for the tobacco warehouse, for by 1750 a mill, storage facilities, houses, and inns had sprung up in colonial Occoquan.

By 1810, the facility now known as the Occoquan Inn not only was operating, the actual building had been reconstructed at least once. The building had been a tavern or inn since the colonial era, a time when the Doeg Indians still flourished in Virginia. At the start of the seventeenth century, the Doeg people lived near what is now known as Prince William Forest Park as part of the Powhatan chiefdom, one of the largest and most powerful tribal bodies encountered by European colonists in Virginia during the late 1500s and early 1600s. At its zenith, the Powhatan paramountcy encompassed over thirty tribes and nearly 6,000 square miles with the major Doeg homeland located where the Fort Belvoir Army base is today (the name "Occoquan" is even a Doeg word meaning "at the end of the water").

The legend of the Occoquan ghost goes back to when the Indians and colonists lived peaceably, so peaceably that the tavern owner employed an Indian. However, it was sex that broke the peace of the tavern. Apparently the Indian and the innkeeper's wife became involved in a love affair, and the innkeeper caught the Indian descending the stairs from the living quarters. The Indian was obviously coming from the wife's bedroom, causing the innkeeper to draw his gun and shoot the Indian, who was dead by the time he landed at the bottom of the steps.

The Fireplace

All that remains of the original residence is the rugged brick fireplace. The ghost who now haunts the inn is thought to be the unfortunate Indian—whose name has been lost to history—because of the first sighting of the spirit, said Sandra Fair, the Occoquan Inn's general manager. That first sighting occurred when smoke rose out from the fireplace. The people who witnessed the smoky spirit described it as having Indian-like features, she said. In addition, the death of the Indian had to have occurred in the 1700s, because there weren't too many Indians left in Virginia by 1810 when the building was reconstructed around the fireplace, she said.

The brick fireplace where the first sighting of the Inn's randy spirit occurred.

Sex and Death in Occoquan

Since the time of the fireplace sightings, most subsequent sightings have involved young women, which is not surprising considering why the Indian was killed, she added. The most common occurrences possibly involving the ghost are reported by the inn's female staff, said Fair, who has been an inn employee for five years. "We've felt a presence, specifically young women who work at the restaurant," she said. At night, while clearing a table, there have been reports of women feeling someone blowing on them. The last one thought it was someone playing a game—the staff likes to kid around a lot—and when she turned around there was no one there. But she said she both felt it on her neck and heard it.

"Late at night, when I'm here, out of the corner of my eye, I've actually seen someone," Fair said. "But when I turn to look, they aren't there anymore. I've seen someone who is tall, with long hair, and with a quilt." A month after Ms. Fair saw what she describes as "the presence," another employee reported seeing the same presence. I hadn't said anything to her about what I saw, or even that I saw anything. "She described a person with long hair, with a quilted vest. In both instances, what was seen was out of the corner of our eyes, and within an instant was gone. But she described the exact same thing I saw."

While the majority of encounters with the ghost tend to be limited to the spiritual equivalent of flirting, there have been reports of touching and what could be anger on the part of the spirit, according to Ms. Fair.

There was one incident with a customer, who is also the town clerk, who was using the ladies room, Ms. Fair said. There is a curtain by the sink where restroom supplies are stored. The female customer was standing in front of the sink, when she said she felt a breeze on her legs. She then felt something grab one of ankles. She looked down and there was nothing there. She was so shocked, that she came and found Ms. Fair that night.

The second incident reveals that the spirit can also have a temper. "I believe that he's not a mean ghost and because I'm here a lot late at night, he looks out for me," Ms. Fair said. But there was one incident that reveals him as maybe a little bit mean, she added. Before the wait staff leaves every night, the two men's and ladies restrooms are cleaned, the doors to the restrooms are left opened. Checking to ensure that the lights and fans are turned off in both restrooms is a chore that is preformed by whoever is on duty each night, she said. This incident involved a woman who was the manager on duty, and she went up to the second floor of the inn. After turning out the lights in the ladies room, she went to the men's room, and oddly found the door was closed. When she tried to open it, she found it wouldn't open. The restroom doors can be locked from the hall, but when she checked, she found it wasn't locked, but the door wouldn't move. "She said that when she pulled on the door, it felt like someone was on the other side pulling back," Fair said. The woman was a big girl, and she kept pulling on the door and eventually managed to get it open enough so she could get a hand in to switch on the light. But, once she got her hand through the opening she was able to create, the door closed on her arm, Ms. Fair said. She was able to pull her arm free, and she had bruises when the door closed on her hand. "It made us [the staff] wonder, but we've never had any type of scares," Ms. Fair said.

However, most incidents involving the Occoquan Inn ghost are of a more playful nature, said Ms. Fair, who adds she was the focus of such a playful incident. "It was my first month here," and it was late one night and there was one more chore to perform— fill the salt and pepper shakers—but she decided it could wait until morning. When Ms. Fair arrived at the inn the next morning, the tops had been removed from all the salt and pepper shakers and were left sitting on the table, she said. "I thought the owner was trying to make a point about ensuring the chores are complete before leaving for the night," she said. So Ms. Fair said to the owner, "If you want to make a point, just tell me. You didn't have to do that."

He responded that he'd just arrived at the inn and did not know what she was talking about.

The inn's owner adamantly denies having anything to do with the removal of the tops from the salt and pepper shakers, and it could only have been done overnight, but no one was in the inn at the time, so none of the staff could have done it, Ms. Fair says.

A List of Occoquan Hauntings

The Occoquan Inn is not the only establishment or dwelling that is home to a spirit in Occoquan. At least ten other buildings are reported to have a ghostly guest. The facilities and highlights about each haunting are:

312 Commerce Street. This dwelling has an active ghost who is known to change the thermostat and unscrew light bulbs.

206 Mill Street. An eighteenth century home where tent shows and circuses were commonly held during the nineteenth century. A ghost named "Charlotte" makes her presence known whenever new merchandise arrives at the shops there. Charlotte is known for rearranging objects and leaving flowers behind.

302 Mill Street. Leary's Lumber and Hardware Store was built in the 1860s and the old sales counter still sits in the front window. The counter is said to be used by the unnamed ghost, but only after regular business hours.

307 Mill Street. A candle is the sign of the ghost at that address.

309 Mill Street. That building was at one time Occoquan's funeral parlor. It is now a retail outlet at which ghostly footsteps have been reported in areas where no one was around.

313 Mill Street. The bricks used to construct the building at that location were made in England and originally used as ballast on a ship. The structure is now a retail outlet at which footprints and rearranged goods are reported to have been left by ghosts, and otherworldly whispers have been heard.

406 Mill Street. A female ghost is believed to haunt the dwelling, but she does not make her presence known often.

410 Mill Street. At that location is a mansion known as "Rockledge" that was built by industrialist John Balladine. Work on Rockledge began in 1758 and the ghost that haunts

the dwelling is believed to be a Confederate soldier.

201 Union Street. Located at the corner of Union and Mills Streets, "The Courtyard" is considered to be haunted by a "silent ghost" who seeks quiet and has taken down chimes to achieve it.

204 Washington Street. This structure is one of the youngest buildings in Occoquan reported to be haunted. Built in 1910, several active ghosts are believed to reside there.

Chapter

10

The Virginia Scientific
Research Association

The Virginia Scientific Research Association (VSRA) is not a group of "ghost busters, psychics or mediums." VSRA was founded in Leesburg, Virginia, by the late Joe ("Ghost Guy") Holbert to do two things: operate ghost tours and find explanations for alleged hauntings. Joe Holbert—who wrote a book, *To Boo, or Not To Boo*—started the VSRA for the same reason something is always started in America, to make money, said Keeler, the association's vice president, who likes to go by one name.

Joe Holbert was a scientist and he started VSRA because he decided there was no such thing as ghosts and he wanted to know what was wrong with people who had those experiences, Keeler said. Mr. Holbert worked on debunking the notion of ghosts and haunting, and he established the VSRA "to keep the new aged, right-sided, intuition-gifted, out of the information trail, [and] to keep their [the organization's] work totally scientific," she said. Mr. Holbert came up with the idea for ghost tours in Leesburg to fund the VSRA, and to find out where residents believed hauntings were taking place, he put out an ad for stories and legends. He expected to hear from a few crackpots, but he didn't expect to hear from judges, preachers, doctors, and other respectable citizens, all providing him with a lot of paranormal stuff happening in their houses. There were over 150 sites alleging paranormal activity around Leesburg alone. All of those alleged haunting didn't sit well with Mr. Holbert, who was a member of the skeptic society. He had never had a paranormal experience, so Mr. Holbert gathered a group of people, including his girlfriend, friends, a plumber, an electrician, and a photographer, and anyone else who was willing to help, to work as a group to debunk the 152 sites. What happened next was the highly disciplined scientific research team of the VSRA used state of the art electromagnetic field (EMF) sensors, computers, and imaging equipment to debunk 110 of the sites where alleged paranormal activity occurred, leaving forty-two that couldn't be explained. That still didn't sit right with Mr. Holbert. "The ghost tours were one thing, they were a money-making endeavor for Leesburg, but

Joe got tired of people having paranormal experiences when he was not experiencing anything," she said.

Because of the high number of sites, it shouldn't be surprising that they were as varied in their locations and the structures are in Leesburg. There are ghosts in a church—the Presbyterian Church, which is haunted by the spirit of a Sunday school teacher named Liza Jenkins, who interacts with the school children—the court house, and in retail and office outlets, Keeler said. There is a retail outlet in Leesburg that changes owners often, she added. At one time it was a pet store called "The Cat House," which allowed customers to take their cats and dogs into the building. People found that the cats would paw at the air as if someone were there, and meow, and the dogs would roll over like they were getting their bellies rubbed. In addition, Keeler says all museums are haunted, but they are not haunted by the spirits of people, they are haunted by the artifacts on display. For example, King Tut cannot be in ten places, even if he's dead, but something he owned can be a containment article for an EMF. In addition to museums, all taverns are haunted as well as all hospitals, jail houses, women's dormitories, and mental wards, she said. Interestingly enough, men's dormitories are not necessarily haunted, the reason being women are more emotional, and men don't tend to expel emotions the way women do, she said.

Mr. Holbert began to conduct research and he contacted people like Keeler, who claims to be a "sensitive," and can therefore "see dead people." The VSRA wanted to know what was wrong with people like Keeler. "So they got together and took a survey where they asked questions like what is your hair color? What is your eye color? What is your nationality? What is your religious belief? How were you raised? Where were you raised? Are you an alcoholic? Are you psychotic? "When I got with Joe, I was a test subject," she said.

As he was conducting his research, one of his interview subjects asked him what time it was because she had another appointment. His response was it is time to buy a watch, but she replied that she had whole box of watches that didn't work. They did not last with her, and the more expensive the watch, the quicker it would stop working, Keeler recounted. The interview subject thought it was a problem with batteries, and Mr. Holbert asked if she would provide him with the box. She did and he sent the box of watches to a local jeweler with the question, what's wrong with these watches? The jeweler said that, first of all, the metal is slightly magnetized, and the batteries were dead. "I'm not a good person to deal with electronics," Keeler said. "But when something stops working, and the batteries are 'dead', they are never fully drained, they usually have some energy left, but not in the watch batteries supplied to Joe," she said. We know that everyone has a human EMF. It is caused by blood circulating and the brain firing synapses, she said. "When you're slow, it's slower, and when you're feeling good it's higher. About eighty-five percent of the population generate from between 40 millivolts to 90 millivolts (a millivolt is one thousandth of a volt). The people who are reporting activity and who can't wear a watch, their activity is between 90 millivolts and 200 millivolts."

This explains why some people leave what are called "residual" impressions, or residual ghosts, Keeler said. "I was at an investigation one day, I had nothing to do, I was bored, and I was playing with the equipment [an EMF meter]," she said. "What I found was a human electromagnetic field moving without a human. It moved and it didn't just move back and forth, it moved as I followed it. It went up the stairs, through the doorway then back through the living room. It showed intelligence. It didn't walk through walls, it didn't disappear," said Keeler, who used the EMF meter to pursue it. Joe Holbert joined her in tracking the residual, and using another EMF meter, they approached it from two angles. Since that first encounter, the VSRA has found millions of residuals. They believe such residue to be a lower EMF activity and will repeat over and over again, she said. There is no intelligence. The scientists in the field, found that to achieve the increased output takes extra electromagnetic field, and the person who is exhibiting increased emotions will turn on a generator and create a power source for the residuals. When someone hits 42 hertz in their brain activity, they are panicking and in "fight or flight," she said. They have all that energy and probably feel like they will explode, so they leave some of that memory at the spot where the increased emotions occurred. We know that when the head is decapitated from the body, as in the case of the headless horseman, the head will still think for up to five minutes. "It still sees, hears and tastes, and if someone is having an experience like seeing their body ride away on a horse, what's left of their head will explode with emotions and their brain will produce the chemicals, and EMF to produce a mark that is left behind. Once the pattern has been set, the result is the headless horseman doing the same thing over and over again," she said.

In addition to residuals, a second type of ghost is the "sentient (or intelligent)," which show a higher EMF range, Keeler said. Emotions are what tie all this together. Sentient ghosts are connected to people they emotionally have some attachment to, while residuals are left behind because someone was emotional, and usually the only people who can see it are emotional individuals, she said. A right brained person, who might be making use of both left and right areas of their brains, are extremely intuitive, and if they are of the same frequency, they'll see what's there, she said.

However, there are exceptions as to where some EM fields are located, such as with a church, Keeler says. EM fields will manifest themselves in other ways. Residual EM fields are usually sound, or visual; however, when extreme EM fields are present, they can actually cause movement, she said. Nonetheless, Keeler would not expect EM field movement in a church, "even through churches can have extreme emotion, but I would expect that type of emotion to be in a jailhouse," she said. Ghost investigators can expect the emotional energy of an EM field to keep getting higher until, after so many days, or whatever time span is needed, some type of activity occurs that causes the energy to be depleted.

Keeler also addresses why ghosts are normally seen at night, or in the dark. "It's not really that apparitions can't be

seen during the day, its peoples' senses," she said. If someone loses their sight, their hearing becomes more in tune.
That is the concept behind being able to see ghosts in the
dark. If a room is dark, people compensate and they become
very aware of every sound, and every glint, she said. For that
reason, it might be better to ghost hunt at night. However,
another reason might be that when you are trying to focus in
on something during the day, there are distractions, including outside noise, that have to be contended with. But one of
the biggest problems with nighttime ghost hunting is that a
person's imagination can turn a coat in a corner into a figure.
"If you're taking away one of your senses (reduced sight), your
imagination may try to fill in the blanks," she said. "That's
why I'll take a child's description [of a ghost] over an adult's,
because an adult will say I saw a woman wearing a large skirt,
and blouse that covers the neck, so she must have been from
the Civil War era. A child will says, she was like mommy, but
she had her hair really tight. With that interview we can get
a lot more information and find out it doesn't have any thing
to do with the Civil War era," she said.

Keeler also explains why some ghosts appear to be clothed.
Residuals are clothed exactly how they saw themselves. "If you
leave a memory—a chemical water mark—that is a residual,
when you are viewed, the residual will be wearing what the
person who made the residual was wearing at the time it was
made," she said. If it is a sentient, we have noticed the women
are younger and skinnier than their last photo, and men always have more hair than their last photo. An example among
the living occurs when people look at photos of themselves,
and say, "Is that me?" Because of that, "we believe how we see
ghosts is how they want us to see them. We think it's a warm
memory they have of themselves."

Chapter 11

I See Dead People

The Virginia Scientific Research Association's (VSRA) vice president is a woman who goes by one name, Keeler, and who says she is among the fifteen percent of humans who actually experience other people's emotions whether they are alive, dead or a memory. That has served her well with the VSRA, which she has been a part of since 1992. She became active in the group because she "wanted to know why some things happen to me and not my friends. Their excuse is they don't believe. I had a lot of people who believe and still can't experience anything." Keeler claims to have seen dead people all her life, and that she was taught as a young child that having visions and knowing things that she couldn't have known was normal and natural. Being sensitive to others' emotions was always treated as "not that big of a deal," said Keeler, who says she still possesses the sensitivity most often seen in young children. How it affects the living is now her calling, which is why VSRA is in its own class, she said. Other groups do not seem to do much with their investigations. They go ghost touring, ghost chasing, yet the members seem to be just trying to find something to do, she said. What the VSRA does that is different from other ghost investigation groups is that the association is dedicated to establishing the science behind "what a true haunting is," rather than determining that a dwelling, or location, is haunted.

Keeler explains that it is her electromagnetic field (EMF) that picks up the frequencies of other EM fields. "I'm like a crystal, like a receiver, and I transmit and receive messages all the time," she said. "My theory is if a person's brain is working on a particular brain-wave frequency, and they run into a ghost that is of an EM field of the same frequency, the living person is going to see the dead person." Most people have some type, or level, of intuitive ability, but they ignore it until it is needed she said. They pick up messages and it is up to each person's ability to reason and deduce what the signal is saying in order to react, she says. An example is when someone walks down a dark alley late at night. "Sometimes they'll be paranoid, but sometimes you know that there's danger about," she says.

"When my EM field comes across another EM field and it picks up a transmission, my brain may go off like an alarm," she said. "If I see something that's 'see through,' it's a residual. It may not even be the memory that's there, but may be the memory of forces that are reenacting a Civil War battle. My brain will go where there is a reenactment right in front of you," she said.

"If I see a sentient, it's usually those times I swear there's someone standing right next to me," Keeler said. Because the brain refreshes every seven seconds just like a computer does, a person's brain-wave frequency changes every seven seconds. "When you feel refreshed and your energy changes and your feelings change. When I hear a sentient, it's usually a holler [trying to attract my attention], but it could be a residual, I'm never sure, until I feel something. Then I know it's a sentient standing behind me wishing he or she could knock me in the back of the head because I've heard my name," she said.

Because she "sees dead people," that has resulted in her getting phone calls at 2 a.m. from people who say they are seeing ghosts, but who aren't, yet who are convinced they are, and many are upset, Keeler says. One of my worst experiences involved a "top dollar lawyer" from Washington, D.C. who was much respected in her field, Keeler said. The woman's husband was trying to have her committed, and we were approached to help with her defense to show she wasn't crazy. Because there is a lot of misunderstanding of mental illness and what is going on, ghost investigators do go to the defense of a lot of people, Keeler said. "I spent three months sitting up with her all night long, and every little flitter from light, like in a reflection from someone's glass, that was an entity to her, and it was watching her," she said. The woman would stay up and videotape her children for hours at night, and if one of the children would reach up and scratch themselves, she would claim that an entity just touched the child, Keeler said. "I would tell her 'no, that wasn't a ghost,' but the woman would not listen. She insisted she was 'not crazy'," Keeler said. That is why the VSRA doesn't charge money to do ghost investigations. "Because we don't charge, I don't have to tell them what they want to hear. In that case, there may have been some low paranormal activity, because there was a teen-age daughter present, but the woman wasn't willing to listen to science, she thought there was no science behind it at all, and it turned into paranoia. We finally had to leave because there was nothing we could do to persuade her that the ghosts were in her imagination," Keeler said.

Emotion Is the Link

Emotions are what ties all this together; a lot of "sensitive" people are susceptible to becoming alcoholics or drug addicts, Keeler says. A lot of their increased risk [relative to non-sensitive people] for substance abuse has to do with not understanding the emotions they have, she says. They do not understand that sentient ghosts are attached to people because they emotionally love you, or they have some emotional attachment. Residuals are left because someone was emotional, and usually the only people who can see it are the emotional ones, who use the right side of their brains the most. For those who wonder when intuitive powers get activated—for women—it's usually when they have a baby, because those mothers need to know when something is wrong with the baby and what they need to do for them. It also lets them know when men may be up to something, or the fact that there's something wrong with a sibling on the other side of the country.

When the VSRA gets a call of poltergeist activity, it is usually slight movement, mostly objects coming off of walls, so the first question asked is, "Is your teenager a boy or girl, and how old is he or she?" Half the time the answer is, "How'd you know we have a teenager?"

Keeler says she speaks from experience because when she was a teenager there were paranormal events that she now says were likely due to her abilities manifesting. "I'd show up at home complaining about the bad day I had at school, and I'd go stomping through the kitchen. All of a sudden the dishes would fall and my parents would ask what happened? I would deny touching them, but what I believed happened in those situations is the dishes shifted a little bit causing them to all fall over because of the emotional energy I would be giving out," she said. In many hauntings, the association has found that most of the time the activity is caused by a teenage girl's emotional energy that is so pent up, that when it gets released it does so in a spectacular fashion. Before the age of seven, both brain hemispheres are one, but at age seven the hemispheres start to separate, and most people generally become more left brain, or right brain dominant, she said. However, if those connections stay joined, the person becomes cross wired, which is the ultimate state to be in because they can use both sides of their brains equally, she said. If the hemispheres of a brain stay joined, and the person is male, he will be more emotional, which usually gets him categorized as artistically talented, she said.

Some men have sympathy pains paralleling those of their pregnant significant other. In addition, a person could be severely depressed and if the depressed person is immediately next to a sensitive individual, that could cause the sensitive to also become depressed, Keeler said. In some cases, the sensitive person becomes so severely depressed that doctors believe there is a chemical imbalance within the sensitive person because the physicians can't find anything wrong in their world. But the problem is, it is not the sensitive's world that is messed up, it is someone who they interact with. That is because some people are constant receivers, they could be described as "broadband" and they are sitting in the middle of all those frequencies. "They hear all the voices, they hear all the emotions, and they can't control anything." If someone is extremely sensitive, they can walk by a group of people and just know who is happy, who is sad, who is depressed, who is euphoric. By the time they get to the end of their day, those people are bipolar, and no one can tell them why. "I usually find in my counseling that when someone is sad or depressed and they don't know why they feel like they do, they usually are empathic. I am not a psychic. Just because I see dead people, I don't say I'm a psychic or a medium. I'm an empath. I feel people whether they are alive, dead or a memory," Keeler said. A problem for Keeler—and others like her—is during high school she felt the emotions of those around her. More than a decade into her marriage, Keeler's husband was depressed, and it transferred to her. "I thought I was mental. I found out I wasn't. Now, if I'm having a panic attack, and I have nothing going on in my life, I'll turn to whomever's feelings I think I'm receiving and ask them, why are you making my brain go through fight or flight? What is going on in your life that is causing me to feel like I'm having a heart attack, because I can't figure out what this is," she said.

Children and lovers leave residuals, and occasionally Keeler will see such a residual out of the corner of her eye. "But there are times when there is so much energy it puts me on overload. When that happens, I can't drive. Because when I'm not on shut down, I know when someone is going to cut in front of me without a blinker. I just simply back off and let them come in. Or if I feel someone anxious and needing to get to work, I'll move out of the way. That is why children will see ghost hands coming at them. In those situations, someone was crying and there is a hand memory at the location. It's also why they see feet under the bed. Someone was sitting on the bed, crying and looking down at their feet. They leave that residual behind and the kids can see it," she said.

Chapter

12

Hauntings in Leesburg

The community of Leesburg, Virginia—situated between Maryland and West Virginia, thirty-five miles northwest of Washington, D.C.—has a population of about 38,500, but there's no data on how many ghosts are in residence there. Home to the Virginia Scientific Research Association (VSRA), Leesburg is also rumored to have a two lane road underneath it that goes from Washington, D.C. to Mount Weather in West Virginia, the location where the top officials in the federal government would be evacuated to in a national emergency. The rumor began when the floor of a Leesburg restaurant started to cave in, and the contractors who were hired to go under the establishment and fix it took some of Leesburg's residents into the tunnel. Among the Leesburg residents taken into the tunnel was VSRA's vice president, Keeler, who said she hates to disappoint peoples' imaginations, but it is not an underground city, only a tunnel painted brown and yellow and wide enough for two cars.

The "Seek" Girl

Leesburg is peppered with dozens of hauntings, including the famous "Seek!" girl. Located at 4 Loudoun Street, in 1972 the sighting of the Seek Girl became one of the most well known ghost sightings in Leesburg. At the location is an office building and the top part of the structure is a facility where National Geographic employees' catalogue photographs for the organization. At the time of the incident, the photos being catalogued were of Civil War heroes, and political leaders, and they are still available for viewing by visitors, but are displayed in a professional museum manner. The area in question is a storage area, and the employees—all women—were working on the top floor of the building when they were visited by a little girl for the first time. The witnesses described the girl as being about three years old, with long blond hair, wearing a little nightgown. The girl was seen peeking through the open part of a doorway when she suddenly yelled, "Seek!" and ran away. By the time the workers recovered from the shock,

The "Seek" Girl was sighted at 4 Loudoun Street, Leesburg.

they went to look for the girl, and, of course, they didn't find her. They also didn't immediately report the visit by the girl because they had some wine with lunch and did not want to be thought of as either drunk on the job or crazy. However, two weeks later the women workers saw the girl for a second time. She was again peeking through the open doorway, and she yelled, "Let's play hide and seek!" This time the workers jumped out of their chairs to follow her, but the girl had disappeared by the first landing. This ghost has come to be thought of fondly among the employees working at the site, and while subsequent sighting have been scarce, the people of Leesburg still like to talk about the girl who yelled, "Seek!"

Peek-A-Boo

Another favorite ghost of Leesburg—thought to be a sentient—is at 17 Loudoun Street, also known as the Benjamin Thornton House. Today a mortgage company occupies the building, and the ghost who inhabits the building is nicknamed "Peek-A-Boo," because every time there has been a sighting of her, she has been seen peeking around corners. Peek-A-Boo also has a coffee addiction, because she has been seen with her hand wrapped around other people's coffee cups. The building at 17 Loudoun Street is another of those Leesburg structures that seems to change hands every six months because of the paranormal activity. At the request of the occupant

The ghost known as "Peek-A-Boo" resides at 17 Loudoun Street, Leesburg.

at the time—a realtor, whose three female employees thought their medication was causing them to hallucinate—the VSRA conducted the first investigation into the haunting. The association did not know much about Peek-A-Boo other than she was reported to be about thirty-five, about five feet tall, had long hair, wore an empire style nightgown, and wasn't wearing shoes, jewelry or makeup. Once the investigation got underway, it was discovered that all three of the workers were seeing the same woman. So VSRA investigators traveled to the town hall to find out if there was a death at the building at any time in its history. But, there were no records of anyone having died there, and there were not any indications that the building had ever been used as a Civil War amputee area like a lot of the other buildings in Leesburg.

However, the VSRA did find out that the building has almost always been some type of a business, except on one occasion when it was owned by a family who used it as a home. So the investigation seemed stalled until 1999 when an older woman who was on a ghost tour claimed to know who Peek-A-Boo was. The elderly woman said she had lived across the street from the dwelling, and when she was much younger she would have cucumber sandwiches and tea with the Peek-A-Boo girl. The woman said she remembered her very well, and proceeded to described Peek-A-Boo perfectly. However, the elderly woman could not remember Peek-A-Boo's real name, except that it had to do with a flower. In addition, the elderly woman said Peek-A-Boo did not die at the building, but at Loudoun County Hospital. So the investigators asked if there was any trauma or abuse at the location, and the woman said she did not know of any. The investigator then asked if Peek-A-Boo was buried close by, and the woman said, as far as she knew, the girl was buried in Cincinnati, Ohio, with the rest of her family. At that point, the VSRA staff was ready to stop trying to understand why Peek-A-Boo remained at 17 Loudoun Street, but the woman provided an answer. The girl died of cancer at a time when very little was known about the disease, she said. It turned out that Peek-A-Boo was married and had a sister who lived in Leesburg at the time Peek-A-Boo was dying. Peek-a-Boo's husband took her back to Leesburg so she couild be with her sister when she died. While it was sad she was dying, the woman whose ghost is known as Peek-A-Boo made it clear that when she was in Leesburg she felt loved and that she wanted to end her life there. Why Leesburg held such a special place for Peek-A-Boo is not known, but the need for love is why her spirit remained, Keeler said. There are only seven known sentient ghosts in Leesburg that are not attached to loved ones, Peek-A-Boo being one of them. When they are attached to a place, it is usually out of patriotism, out of a passion for something, or out of the fact they felt loved at the location, and never because they wanted to get back at someone, Keeler added.

The Tavern and the Law Firm

There have been at least eight attempts to operate a tavern at the lower rear of 19 East Market Street. The problem is, the spirit activity is so high there that people just get tired of picking up bits and pieces of equipment and other tavern materials every morning. The VSRA has learned that every time there's a high electromagnetic field (EMF) going on, the video cameras used to track ghosts will not work well at the lower part of 19 East Market Street because the EM fields there drain the batteries. Therefore, whenever someone conducts a ghost investigation and they plan on using video equipment, they need to have about twelve battery packs.

Because taverns are always haunted, said Keeler, she has concluded that drinking establishments attract ghosts because a fair number of saloon customers are likely to have substance abuse problems. Some of them might be dysfunctional people in different aspects of their lives, but many are also very sensitive people who can handle a lot of emotional downloading, she said. Musicians who play in bars, or the wait staff and bartenders, usually are good at reading people. They can get into the groove with customers, and many can take one look

Spirit activity has thwarted at least eight attempts to open a tavern in the lower rear of 19 East Market Street, Leesburg.

at someone and tell if they are a beer, wine or liquor drinker. In addition, because they are sensitive, they also go into fields such as counseling or health care, because "their specialty is doing people."

It is emotional people who usually go into bars, Keeler said. That's why bars are always haunted, and every time a tavern has opened up on the lower level of 19 East Market Street, Leesburg's "emotional people gather together" and start drinking alcohol. That is when the activity is known to have started. There may not even be a sentient in the lower level of the building, it may just be one giant residual haunting. With all the customers and staff drinking and sharing emotional activity, there is a lot of energy building up. What happens there is the EM field in the tavern section increases greatly, the bar closes, everyone goes home, and the built up energy has to disperse. So it acts like a little flare and it exhausts its own energy. While it is not likely that a sentient ghost resides in the lower level of 19 East Market Street, the upper level—which houses a law firm—might have two sentient ghosts in residence.

There is a room on the top floor of 19 East Market that is used only for conferences because the EM fields in the room disrupt the office equipment, so the firm just reserves the room for conferences. That is where the building's two sentient ghosts, a father and son, are believed to be primarily located. In addition, the firm has another apparition, likely a residual, who sits at the doorway. Keeler has seen the residual. It occurred in 1993, when Keeler was working as a child advocate. It was her first case, and she went running up the stairs of the law firm, entered the doorway, looked across, and the female apparition was near the doorway. She was sitting, wearing a black dress, with a black veil, and she was crying into her own

But spirit activity is business as usual in the upper part of 19 East Market Street, Leesburg.

hands. Keeler searched the law firm for someone to inform, and told them there is a woman downstairs crying. The firm's employees asked if she was dressed in black with a veil? When Keeler responded in the affirmative, they said, the spirit was always there. That surprised Keeler because it was coming from a building full of lawyers. The firm's employees were admitting they could see the dead woman in the corner. Keeler then investigated the haunting and is convinced the woman in black is a residual of someone else seeing her crying. If the woman herself were the source of the residual energy, the residual would be hands. There's a chance the woman was crying because she may have just been evicted from her home due to the death of her husband. The shutters and doors on 19 East Market Street are original. We know that because they are painted black, or have been over painted. During the Civil War, all of Leesburg's men between the ages of eighteen to thirty-three went to war. And at one horrific battle, all the men from Leesburg were wounded, killed or declared missing within three days. As a result, every woman in Leesburg painted the homes' doors black to show they were in mourning, and the widows were about to be evicted from their homes because women could not own property. As soon as a man was killed, lawyers would inform the widow that she would have to vacate the dwelling. Many of the women of Leesburg would show up at a lawyer's office, like that at 19 Market Street, to fight for their right to live in their homes, hence, the strong emotions.

Court House Ghosts

The Leesburg Court, located at 18 East Market Street, is supposedly haunted by a slave named Mercer, who during the Civil War killed the man who owned him. Because he killed the slave owner, Mercer was set upon by a mob that hung him until dead, decapitated him, impaled his head on a pole, and quartered his body, scattering pieces of him throughout Leesburg as a warning to other slaves. Because of that great injustice to Mercer, some of Leesburg's judges believe he haunts the

Leesburg's judges believe a slave named Mercer, who was executed by a mob, haunts the town's court house at 18 East Market Street.

courthouse. However, Keeler doubts that is the case. There is a place in the court called the "barristers' bench;" it is the table where all the accused sit. The defendants sit there worried for their lives, their families, their money, and whether they are going to lose their freedom, and all that emotion is going into the wood table, she said. So when something on the barristers' bench moves a couple of inches—like a glass of water, or a piece of paper—the court will document it as "Mercer." Those who serve on juries at the court are told not to be surprised if something paranormal happens, and not to pay attention to any movement or to bring it up if it happens, she adds.

In addition, there is a tree on the court house and municipal grounds that has an active residual field. The VSRA conducted its investigation around Leesburg in 1993, and it took the association sixteen months to either debunk or document the paranormal. One of the strongest residual fields found was on the grounds of the Leesburg Municipal complex. It was reported that an apparition of a man was running through the municipal grounds, and either someone was chasing him or he was chasing something. From ten percent to fifteen percent of the population will feel the residual where the apparition was seen, Keeler said. A candle vigil was held on the grass there, and Keeler deduced that if residuals are the result of highly charged emotions, there should be leftover energy at the site. There was an investigation of the area where the vigil took place and an EM field of about 35 millivolts was recorded. That was "one of the strongest fields I ever found that wasn't in the kill zone of a battle field," she said. This is a place of great emotion and it's still there.

As part of the research for this book, I took up Keeler's offer and approached the Leesburg municipal grounds near the tree where the vigil was held, and under Keeler's instruction held my hand up and extended my arm. I immediately felt two pinprick shocks—which felt like static electricity—on the middle finger and third finger of my right hand. The strange thing was, I wasn't touching anything, or near anything or

Leesburg's Municipal Grounds has an active residual field on the King Street side, adjacent to the large tree on the left side of the photo.

anyone. I was holding my hand up to the air. I would have determined the pinprick shocks to be some sort of static electricity, but about two seconds after feeling the shocks, there was a feeling that something was pushing against the palm of my right hand. It felt substantial and hard, yet there was nothing there. A second or two later, the middle toe of my right foot felt a squeezing which turned into a full pinch. My toe persisted to feel as if it were being pinched for several more minutes, even after I left the municipal grounds. The feeling of being pinched remained as I walked to where I parked my automobile, and it did not leave my toe until I drove out of Leesburg. Prior to entering Leesburg that evening my shoes fit fine with no discomfort. I have worn those shoes since the visit to Leesburg and have not experienced any further pinching. I cannot explain why my toe would feel as it were being pinched at that particular moment.

Chapter 13

Ball's Bluff Haunting

In the northeast corner of Leesburg, Virginia, is the Ball's Bluff Battlefield and National Cemetery, located just off the Route 15 Bypass north, which is the site of Loudoun County's largest Civil War battle. It was a small skirmish when compared to other battles—nearby Manassas for example—but to Civil War historians it lingers as a monument to deadly disorganization, and possibly holds the spirits of Union troops killed there.

The battle of Ball's Bluff was a badly conceived and coordinated attempt by Union forces, commanded by Brig. Gen. Charles P. Stone, to cross the Potomac at Harrison's Island and capture Leesburg. At Gen. Stone's command was a force consisting of the 1st California, the 15th and 20th Massachusetts, the 42nd New York, and three pieces of artillery from New York and Rhode Island, totaling about 1,700 troops. Defending against the Union troops was Confederate Brig. Gen. Nathan Evans, who commanded a force consisting of the 13th, 17th, and 18th Mississippi, and the 8th Virginia, which also totaled about 1,700 troops.

The key point in the battle occurred shortly after dawn on October 21, 1861, when a Union force commanded by Col. Edward D. Baker, a senator from Oregon, crossed the Potomac River and scaled Ball's Bluff with the goal of striking out for Leesburg. The raiders were quickly surrounded by the Confederate forces, who inflicting heavy casualties on the Union troops resulting in 223 dead (including Baker), 226 wounded, and 553 captured. Confederate forces did much better with thirty-six dead, 117 wounded, and only three captured.

The Union was routed at Ball's Bluff, with many of the northern troops attempting to escape the carnage by climbing down or jumping from the steep cliff of the bluff. Other Union troops tried to swim the Potomac to Harrison's Island and they were either shot by Confederates who held the high ground and were able to pick off the Yankees at will, or drowned. Either way, their bodies washed ashore down stream.

The defeat was such bad news for Washington, that within six weeks of the battle, the U.S. Congress created the Joint Committee on the Conduct of the War, in part to discover the causes of that debacle. Mostly for political reasons, the committee blamed General Stone for what more properly were Col. Baker's mistakes. As a result, Gen. Stone was jailed for six months in 1862 and his promising career came to an end. It was a small battle, soon overshadowed by larger, bloodier fights, but the Confederates hailed the battle as a stunning victory, while some humiliated Federals forever referred to the battle as "that cursed Ball's Bluff."

Cursed possibly, for apparitions of soldiers climbing the cliffs have been reported, which is not unusual for Civil War battlefields, says John Warfield, of the DC Metro Area Ghost Watchers. "There are sighting of the spirits of Civil War dead all through the Northern Virginia area," he said. "We get calls on Civil War apparitions regularly, and a lot of the apparitions are residual spirits, a lot are intelligent [spirits]," he said.

In addition to the sightings of apparitions, there are "urban legend" stories of ghosts at Ball's Bluff, with one of the best known reported to have occurred during the 1950s and involved a group of teenagers who went to the bluff and were terrified by screams that filled the air there. According to the legends, the youths ran back to their vehicle, but the auto would not move. The story says the teenagers believed the car was being held in place, but they did not see anyone or anything holding the car. Eventually the car moved, and when the teens made it home, in true urban legend fashion, they discovered muddy handprints on the car.

The story continues with the parents of a teenager then going to the Ball's Bluff cemetery to see if there was anyone there. The story says the parents did not find anything unusual, but when they approached three graves that are located outside the wall of the cemetery, a small tree shook and bent nearly to the ground, scaring the adults into fleeing the cemetery. There is speculation that the screams are from the spirits of the Union troops who were fleeing the Confederate guns.

Colonel Burt

There is another casualty of the Battle of Ball's Bluff, but the soldier did not die at the battlefield and he is believed to haunt a Leesburg building. The spirit of Confederate Colonel Erasmus R. Burt, commander of the 18th Mississippi Infantry, is said to haunt a building now known as Glenfiddich House located at 205 North King Street, Leesburg. Colonel Burt was gravely wounded at the battle and taken to what was then the home of Henry Harrison. While attempts were made to help him recover from his wounds, Colonel Burt died within four days of being taken to the home. Today, the building is a career management company, and managers and employees alike report the sound of marching in the hall outside the second-flood room where Colonel Burt died. In addition, there is a report of a man dressed in a Confederate uniform, complete with plumes, appearing at the second floor hall. The witness said the man was dressed as a Confederate officer and the apparition, like all old soldiers, just faded away.

Bibliography

Foreword
Personal interview with Al Tyas (April 2008)
Personal interview with John Warfield (May 2008)
Research was conducted and notes taken during the following ghost tour: Alexandria's Ghost & Graveyard Tour (July 2008)
Research was conducted and notes taken during a tour of the Carlyle House Historical Park (July 8, 2008)

Chapter 1
"Local News." *Alexandria Gazette* (1868)
Personal interview with Candida Krbb, (July 2008)
Research was conducted and notes taken during the following ghost tour: Alexandria's Ghost & Graveyard Tour (July 2008)

Chapter 2
Personal interview with Diana Bridger (Oct. 7, 2007)
Personal interview with John Warfield (May 2008)
Research was conducted and notes taken during the following ghost tour: Alexandria's Ghost & Graveyard Tour (June 2008)

Chapter 3
Wikipedia, "Gadsby's Tavern Museum": http://en.wikipedia.org/wiki/Gadsby%27s_Tavern_Museum
Research was conducted and notes taken during the following ghost tour: Alexandria's Ghost & Graveyard Tour (Oct. 31, 2006)
Research was conducted and notes taken during a tour of Gadsby's tavern Museum (July 8, 2008)

Chapter 4
Research was conducted and notes taken during a tour of Woodlawn Plantation (August 2008)

Chapter 5
Research was conducted and notes taken during the following
ghost tour: Alexandria's Footsteps to the Past (July 5, 2008)
Research was conducted and notes taken during the following
ghost tour: Alexandria's Ghost & Graveyard Tour (Oct. 31,
2006; June 2008 and July 2008)

Chapter 6
Kendall, Mary Claire. "The Historically significant life of Colo-
nel John Carlyle – That Almost Vanished." *Alexandria Times*
(Nov. 10-17, 2005)
Research was conducted and notes taken during the following
ghost tour: Alexandria's Footsteps to the Past (July 5, 2008)
Research was conducted and notes taken during the follow-
ing ghost tour: Alexandria's Ghost & Graveyard Tour (July
2008)
Research was conducted and notes taken during a tour of the
Carlyle House Historical Park (July 8, 2008)

Chapter 7
Personal interview with Dawn Boutelle (Sept. 7, 2008)
Personal interview with Jan Cunard (Sept. 7, 2008)
Personal interview with John Rossi (Sept. 7, 2008)
Personal interview with John Warfield (Sept. 7, 2008)

Chapter 8
History, Dumfries, Virginia Website: http://www.dumfriesvirginia.
org/history.html
Research was conducted and notes taken during a tour of the
Weems-Botts Museum (August 9, 2008)

Chapter 9
Personal interview with Sandra Fair (July 2008)

Lynn, Martha. "A Brief History of Occoquan" (1975): 3-10.

Occoquan Merchant Association, Inc., "Occoquan Shopping & Dining Guide" (2008): 6-9.

Chapter 10
Research was conducted and notes taken during the following ghost tour: The Virginia Scientific Research Association (Aug. 30, 2008)

Virginia Scientific Research Association Website: http://www.vsra.net/tour.php

Chapter 11
Research was conducted during Virginia Scientific Research Association ghost tour of Leesburg, Va. conducted by Keeler (Aug. 30, 2008)

Virginia Scientific Research Association Website: http://www.vsra.net/tour.php

Chapter 12
Research was conducted and notes taken during the following ghost tour: The Virginia Scientific Research Association (Aug. 30, 2008)

Chapter 13
eHistory Archive, Battle of Balls Bluff: http://ehistory.osu.edu/uscw/features/regimental/pennsylvania/union/71stPennsylvania/ballsbluff.cfm

Nelms, Douglas W. "Ghosts Walk Among the Living in Old Leesburg." *The Washington Times* (Oct. 27, 2005)

Personal interview with John Warfield (Sept. 7, 2008)

Research was conducted and notes taken during the following ghost tour: The Virginia Scientific Research Association (Aug. 30, 2008)